بِسْمِ اللَّهِ الرَّحْمَٰنِ الرَّحِيمِ

IN THE NAME OF ALLAH, THE BENEFICENT, THE MERCIFUL

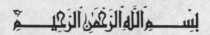

What Is
Ṣalāt (Prayer)?

By:
Martyr Āyatullāh Sayyid M.H. Beheshtī

- *This standing, and bending down;*
- *This way of sitting, and laying the forehead on the ground;*
- *And uttering words in each position,*
- *What does it all mean?*

سرشناسه	: بهشتی ، محمد ، ۱۳۰۷ ـ ۱۳۶۰ . Beheshti , Muhammad .
عنوان قراردادی	: نماز چیست ؟ انگلیسی .
عنوان و نام پدیدآورنده	: What is Salat (prayer) ? By M.H. Beheshti .
مشخصات نشر	: Tehran . 2007 = 1386 , International publishing co .
مشخصات ظاهری	: ۱۲۸ ص . مصور رنگی .
شابک	: 978-964-304-027-7
وضعیت فهرست نویسی	: فیپا .
یادداشت	: انگلیسی .
آوانویسی عنوان	: وات ایز صلات (پریر) ؟ .
موضوع	: نماز ـ راهنمای آموزشی .
شناسامه افزوده	: سازمان تبلیغات اسلامی ، شرکت چاپ و نشر بین الملل .
رده بندی کنگره	: BP ۱۴۷/۷/ ن ۸ ب ۸۰۴۹۵۲ ۱۳۸۶
رده بندی دیویی	: ۲۹۷ / ۳۵۳۰۷
شماره کتابشناسی ملی	: ۱۱۴۸۷۱۱

نماز چیست ؟

شهید بهشتی (انگلیسی)

INTERNATIONAL
PUBLISHING CO.

What is Salat (Prayer) ?
By: M . H . Beheshti
Publisher: International Publishing Co.
Third Published: 1386
Printed and bound by: Sepehr Printing House
In 3000 Copies
ISBN: 978-964-304-027-7
Pric 2000

Contents

Transliteration

Arabic-Persian Alphabet	Key Word	Transliteration Symbols	Examples	English Equivalent	
				Sound	Key Word
ء	رأی	, ra'y	/E/	ago	
ب	قبل	b	qabl	/b/	bad
پ	پل	p	pull	/p/	pen
ت	متن	t	matn	/t/	tea
ث	تمر	th	thamar	/θ/	thin
ج	جبْر	j	jabr	/dʒ/	jump
چ	چاپ	ch	chəp	/tʃ/	chin
ح	حمد	ḥ	ḥamd	—	—
خ	خوف	kh	khawf	—	—
د	درس	d	dars	/d/	do
ذ	ذکر	dh	dhikr	/ð/	then
ر	ربّ	r	rabb	/r/	red
ز	زمان	z	zamān	/z/	zoo
ژ	ژاپن	zh	zhapan	/ʒ/	vision
س	سَبب	s	sabab	/s/	so
ش	شرف	sh	sharaf	/ʃ/	she
ص	صدق	ṣ	ṣida	—	—
ض	ضَعف	ḍ	ḍa'f	—	—
ط	فطْر	ṭ	fiṭr	—	—
ظ	نَظَر		naẓar	—	—
ع	عین		'ayn	—	—
غ	غریب		gharīb	—	—
ف	طرف	f	ṭaraf	/f/	fall
ق	قرآن	q	Qur'ān	—	—
ك	أکبر	k	akbar	/k/	cat
گ	گازی	g	gāzī	/g/	got
ل	هلال	l	hilāl	/l/	leg

Transliteration

Arabic-Persian Alphabet	Key Word	Transliteration Symbols	Examples	English Equivalent	
				Sound	Key Word
م	قوم	m	qawm	/m/	man
ن	نهج	n	nahj	/n/	no
و	قول	w	awl	/w/	wet
ه	هواء	h	hawā’	/h/	how
ي	بيان	y	bayān	/j/	yes
ة	بقية	ah	baqiyyah	—	—
Short Vowels					
ـَ	أَبَد	a	abad	/e//^/	between (bed and bud)
ـُ	هُو	u	huwa	/u/	
ـِ	كَلِمة	i	kalimah	/i/	sit
Long Vowels					
ـَا	رَامَ	ā	rāma	/a:/	arm
ـُو	داوُد	ū	Dāwūd	/u:/	too
ـِي	نِيران	ī	nīrām	/i:/	see
Diphthongs					
ـَوْ	مَوْعد	aw	maw‘id	—	—
ـَيْ	بَيْنَ	ay	bayna	/ei/	page
ـِيّ	أَقَلِيّة	iyy	aqaliyyah	—	—
ـُوّ	قُوّات	uww	quwwāt	—	—
ءَا(آ)	مَآب	’ā	ma’āb	—	—

Publisher's Preface

The present book is a translation of one of the valuable religious books, on the *Ṣalāt* (prayer), its importance, performance and objectives written by martyr Dr. Muhammad Husayn Beheshti — may the Almighty Allah sanctify his soul. He wrote it in Persian, using a concise simple style with expressive phrases and impressive idioms; meanwhile it is covering all the subject effectively, and in a lively practicable method. Moreover the original Persian style is unmatched and trustworthy. In fact it is written by him in 1347 (H-Sh), and has been reprinted several times in Persian.

This English translation of the book is the third edition. Being checked thoroughly with the original revised Persian book, it is fully reviewed, reedited, and many necessary changes and alterations have been made. Furthermore a chart for the transliteration symbols with the Arabic-Persian letters (and examples) has been given at the beginning of the book so as to help the dear readers to thoroughly read the Arabic Islamic words and phrases. At the end of the book a glossary of non-English terms has been given.

It is hoped that this valuable book will help the committed Muslim reader to deepen practicably his faith and practice in the Islamic precepts and teachings.

International Publishing Co.,
Islamic Propagation Organization

In the Name of Allah, the Beneficent, the Merciful

Glorification and Worship

The moment a man thinks of the infinite glory and absolute perfection of Allah, the Creator of the universe, he falls into adoration for Him with all his heart, pays homage with all his body and soul, to the Almighty Allah, bowing down to Him in all humility. Pushed by human nature, his genuflexion, in obedience and reverence to all this perfection and glory of Allah, is called "*rukū'*".

When one touches the ground with one's forehead in prostration, it is called *"sujūd"*. When one praises one's Creator, thanking and glorifying Him, it is called "*ḥamd*" and *"tasbih"*.

Faithful Devotion and Supplication

The moment a man feels in need of help from a supernatural power, superior to matter, he turns towards the Omniscient, the Wise and the Merciful-the Creator of the Universe. He Communes with Him, discloses all his sorrows an desires, and implores His help. This is called *"du'ā'"* (Supplication).

Divine Worship ('Ibādah)

All this glorification, adoration, love, faithful devotion, supplication and prayer to Almighty Allah, is called in the language of the Qur'ān "*'ibādah*" (Divine worship). The Holy Qur'an maintains that this Divine worship is only for Allah, the Unique and the Incomparable, and that the worship of any other being or thing besides Him is strictly forbidden and considered "a great sin" by the Holy Qur'ān:

«وَقَضىٰ رَبُّكَ اَلاّ تَعْبُدُوا اِلاّ اِيّاهُ».

"And your Lord has commanded that you worship none but Him..."

(The Holy Qur'ān, 17:23)

In Islam, from a general viewpoint, no particular language, form or thing has been specified for the general worship of the Unique God, Allah. No specific rule or condition has been stated. The only important thing that must be strictly observed in the Islamic worship is that whatever the worshippers — the servants of Allah-do in the Divine worship must not be polluted by superstition, polytheism, ostentation, hypocrisy or pretence.

Therefore, Muslims, carefully, observing these, can adore Allah Almighty and commune with Him at any time, in any place, and in any language, form or manner they want to.

The *Salāt* (Prayer)

The *Salāt* (Prayer)

The *Salāt* is a specific ritual form for the worship of Allah, and it entails the expression of love and devotion to Him. It contains and associates invaluable and specific instructive aspects. And for this reason, it has a special ritual form for itself.

The Hymn of Monotheism, Virtue and Purity

The *Salāt* is hymn of monotheism, virtue and purity. It helps keep our mind and soul free from the agents of idolatry, polytheism, paganism, and other such pollutions which we face in the course of our daily life.

Each of us works the hardest he can to realise his objectives of his daily life, and rarely he thinks about anything else.

Toiling hard from morning to evening is something quite natural and necessary for man. It gives him vigour and joy in tackling everyday problems. His energy and intellect open up new avenues for his talents. Through his knowledge of arts, science and industry he can make new inventions, which improve his living conditions, and enable him to progress even more. But at the same time, his busy life, his egoism and selfish desires lead him to a stage that now and then, to realise his objectives, he bends and bows to every person, debasing himself. He undermines his self-respect and the true value of his real and human character, and in this manner, pollutes his actual personality, body and soul.

Some Examples of physical pollution

Few are those whose hands and feet, heads and faces, and sometimes even bodies and clothes, do not get dirty at daily work, and thus not require daily cleaning.

For instance, a teacher engaged in teaching students, who reads and writes continuously; farmer or a tiller who ploughs the field, sows the seeds, implants saplings, weeds the garden, irrigates, reaps and harvests the crops; an engineer or a worker who toils in the workshop; a doctor or a nurse who deals with patients; a housewife or a housekeeper who does household work; a merchant or a tradesman, who works at the market-place; a researcher scientist who works in the laboratory or conducts research in his field of specialisation whether in the university atmosphere or in the arena of nature; all need to wash their faces and clothes, or take a bath once or several times daily, in order to remain clean.

Likewise, our souls, are subject to different kinds of pollution; sometimes to a higher degree than that of our physical being, in dealing with others during our daily tasks. Examples of these are those arising from uncontrolled capricious passions and lusts, greed, selfishness, egotism, emulation, taking pride at victory and success, psychological complex resulting from disappointment and defeat; as well as jealousy, envy, enmity, revenge and hundreds of other kinds of pollution.

Such kinds of pollution blacken our souls; cause them to deviate from the right path of life, virtue, purity and piety; give way to depravity and corruption; make one forget all about Allah; and throw one into the devil's trap which encourages one to commit evil.

Cleaning of the Heart and Soul

Therefore, in the same way as we wash and clean our clothes and bodies, we must also spend time in cleaning our hearts and souls.

To attain the pleasure of Allah — The Primary Source of purity and perfection — we must spend some time for remembering and thanking Him, in supplication and sincere prayer. In this way we shall wash our contaminated souls with the pure and limpid water of the Divine Fountain.

This is what *ṣalāt* (ritual prayer) is, which a Muslim performs several times everyday.

It is narrated that the holy prophet (S.A.) had concisely said to his companions:

"Suppose in front of the house of one of you, there is a river, and he washes himself in it five times a day, will there still remain any dirt on his body?" They said. "No, this washing will cleanse the body of all dirt." Then he said, "The five-time *ṣalawāt* (ritual prayers) do the same thing. With these five daily prayers Allah obliterates all one's sins and makes one pure and clean."[1]

Timing of the Daily Ṣalawāt
(Five Ritual Prayers)

Timing of the Daily Ṣalawāt
(Five Ritual Prayers)

1. *Ṣubḥ* (morning): At the dawn or commencement of the morning.
2. *Ẓuhr* (noon): At midday
3. *'Aṣr* (afternoon): About 2 to 3 hours afternoon.[2]
4. *Maghrib* (evening): After sunset.[3]
5. 'Ishā' (night fall): At night when it gets dark.[4]

These are the original timings for performing the *ṣalawāt* (prayers), and it is better that each ritual prayer is performed at the right time. But for each one of the five ritual *ṣalawāt*, extended timing has been fixed so that if a man, because of work or some other constraints, could not perform his *ṣalawāt* at the afore-stated time, he can have more sufficient time at his disposal.

The following is the duration for each *ṣalāt*.

- ❑ *Ṣalātus-Ṣubḥ*: From dawn to sunrise.
- ❑ *Ṣalātuẓ-Ẓuhr*: From midday to sunset.
- ❑ *Ṣalātul-'Aṣr*: After *Ṣalātuẓ-Ẓuhr* until sunset.
- ❑ *Ṣalātul-Maghrib*: From *maghrib* until midnight.[5]
- ❑ *Ṣalātul-'Ishā'*: After *Ṣalātul-Maghrib* until midnight.[5]

When a Muslim gets up in the morning, he performs the *ṣalāt* to enable him commence his daily work with a pure heart, goodwill, and attention towards the Almighty Allah.

At noon, during his lunch break, he temporarily stops his work and again performs the *ṣalāt.* He does so, because as he eats to provide Fresh energy and joy to his body, he enriches and cheers his soul through performing the *Ṣalāt.* Before resuming his job in the afternoon, he performs the *ṣalāt* again so that he may work, with Allah in mind.

After sunset (evening), when it is usually time to stop the daily work and enjoy dinner, he once again performs the *ṣalāt,* so that he may nourish his soul while gratifying his body with food.

At night, when one about to retire to bed, he once again stands up before Allah and performs his *ṣalāt.* So, just as he started the day by remembering and praying to Allah Almighty, he ends it with *ṣalāt* and remembrance of Allah. Thus, he goes to sleep with a comforted soul and a pure heart.

Allah in the Holy Qur'ān says:

«وَاَقِمِ الصَّلٰوةَ طَرَفَيِ النَّهَارِ وَزُلَفاً مِنَ اللَّيلِ اِنَّ الْحَسَنٰاتِ يُذْهِبْنَ السَّيِّئاتِ ذٰلِكَ ذِكْرٰى لِلذّاكِرينَ»

"And keep up the ṣalāt at the two ends of the day and at some parts of the night. Surely, good deeds take away ill deeds. This is a reminder for the mindful."

(The Holy Qur'ān 11: 114)

Adhān — the Call to *Ṣalāt* (Prayer)

Adhān — the Call to *Ṣalāt* (Prayer)

The time for each *ṣalāt* is announced by *adhān*, the proclamation for *ṣalāt.* At dawn, noon, afternoon, after sunset at early evening, and when it starts getting dark, throughout the Islamic regions, the call with the soul-comforting voice of *adhān* is heard by everyone. This call proclaims that it is time for *ṣalāt.*

اَللهُ اَكْبَرُ، اَللهُ اَكْبَرُ. اَللهُ اَكْبَرُ، اَللهُ اَكْبَرُ.

"Allāhu Akbar, Allāhu Akbar, Allāhu Akbar, Allāhu Akbar"
(Allah is the Greatest)

اَشْهَدُ اَنْ لا اِلٰهَ اِلَّا اللهُ. اَشْهَدُ اَنْ لا اِلٰهَ اِلَّا اللهُ.

"Ashhadu an lā ilāha illa-Llāh.
Ashhadu an lā ilāha illa-Llāh."
(I clearly observe and bear witness that there is no god but Allah, [the Creator of the universe].)

اَشْهَدُ اَنَّ مُحَمَّداً رَسُولُ اللهِ. اَشْهَدُ اَنَّ مُحَمَّداً رَسُولُ اللهِ.

"Ashhadu anna Muḥammadan Rasūlu-Llāh.
Ashhadu anna Muḥammadan Rasūlu-Llāh."

(I clearly observe and bear witness that Muḥammad (S.A.) is the Messenger of Allah.)[6]

حَيَّ عَلَى الصَّلٰاة. حَيَّ عَلَى الصَّلٰاةِ

"Ḥayya `alas-Ṣalāh.
Ḥayya `alas-Ṣalāh."
(Hurry up to *Ṣalāt.*)

حَيَّ عَلَى الْفَلٰاح. حَيَّ عَلَى الْفَلٰاح

"Ḥayya 'alā-falāḥ.
Ḥayya 'alā-falāḥ."
(Hurry up to the deliverance)

حَيَّ عَلٰى خَيْرِ الْعَمَل. حَيَّ عَلٰى خَيْرِ الْعَمَلِ

"Ḥayya 'alā Khayril-'amal.
Ḥayya `alā Khayril-`amal."
(Hurry up to the best deed)

اَللّٰهُ اَكْبَرُ. اَللّٰهُ اَكْبَرُ

"Allāhu Akbar.
Allāhu Akbar."
(Allah is the Greatest.)

لَا اِلٰهَ اِلَّا اللّٰهُ. لَا اِلٰهَ اِلَّا اللّٰهُ.

Lā ilāha illa-Llāh.
Lā ilāha illa-Llāh.
(There is no god but Allah.)

Iqāmah — the Recitation (of the Same *Adhān* Phrases with Little Difference) Directly Before *Ṣalāt*

Iqāmah — the Recitation (of the Same *Adhān* Phrases with Little Difference) Directly Before *Ṣalāt*

On hearing *adhān,* the call to prayers, a Muslim prepares himself for *ṣalāt* and comes to the place intended for this purpose. Those who wish to perform congregational prayers (*Ṣalātul-jama`ah*), proceed to the mosque or some other place, which is prepared and arranged in advance for its performance.

At this time, before starting *ṣalāt, iqāmah* is recited as follows:

اَللهُ اَكْبَرُ، اَللهُ اَكْبَرُ.

Allāhu Akbar, Allāhu Akbar.
(Allah is the Greatest)

اَشْهَدُ اَنْ لا اِلٰهَ اِلَّا اللهُ: اَشْهَدُ اَنْ لا اِلٰهَ اِلَّا اللهُ

"Ashhadu an lā ilāha illa-Llāh.
Ashhadu an lā ilāha illa-Llāh."
(I clearly observe and bear witness that there is no god but Allah, [the Creator of the universe].)

اَشْهَدُ اَنَّ مُحَمَّداً رَسُولُ الله. اَشْهَدُ اَنَّ مُحَمَّداً رَسُولُ اللهِ

"Ashhadu anna Muḥammadan Rasūlu-Llāh.
Ashhadu anna Muḥammadan Rasūlu-Llāh."

(I clearly observe and bear witness that Muḥammad (S.A.) is the Messenger of Allah)

حَيَّ عَلَى الصَّلٰوةِ. حَيَّ عَلَى الصَّلٰوةِ

"Hayya `alas-Salāh,
Hayya `alas-Ṣalāh."
(Hurry up to *Ṣalāt.*)

حَيَّ عَلَى الْفَلَاحِ. حَيَّ عَلَى الْفَلَاح

"Ḥayya 'alal-falāḥ.
Ḥayya 'alal-falāḥ."
(Hurry up to the deliverance)

حَيَّ عَلٰى خَيْرِ الْعَمَلِ. حَيَّ عَلٰى خَيْرِ الْعَمَل

Ḥayya 'alā Khayril-'amal.
Hayya `alā Khayril-`amal.
(Hurry up to the best deed)

قَدْ قَامَتِ الصَّلٰوةُ. قَدْ قَامَتِ الصَّلٰوة

Qad qāmatis-ṣalah, Qad qamatis-ṣalah.
(Indeed *Ṣalāt* has started.)

اَللّٰهُ اَكْبَرُ. اَللّٰهُ اَكْبَرُ.

Allāhu Akbar, Allāhu Akbar.
(Allah is the Greatest.)

لَا اِلٰهَ اِلاَّ اللّٰهُ.

Lā ilāha illa-Llāh
(There is no god, but Allah [the Creator of all the worlds])

How to Be Prepared for Ṣalāt.
Perform the ritual ablution (*Wuḍū'*), and then rise up for performing the *Ṣalāt*

Wuḍū' — the Ritual Ablution before *Ṣalāt*

Wuḍū' — the Ritual Ablution before *Ṣalāt*

First wash the face and then, the arms, from the elbows to the fingers; then draw the wet hand, once from the top of the head up to the forehead, and then on the feet.[7]

The Holy Qur'ān says:

يَا اَيُّهَا الَّذِينَ آمَنُوا اِذَا قُمْتُمْ اِلَى الصَّلٰوةِ فَاغْسِلُوا وُجُوهَكُمْ وَاَيْدِيكُمْ اِلَى الْمَرَافِقِ وَامْسَحُوا بِرُؤُسِكُمْ وَاَرْجُلَكُمْ اِلَى الْكَعْبَيْنِ.

"O you who believe! When you rise up for the Ṣalāt, wash your faces and your hands as far as the elbows, and wipe, your heads and feet to the ankles..."

(The Holy Qur'ān 5: 6)

Wuḍū, should be performed with pure *niyyah* (intention), and for the sake of the Almighty Allah.

If any part of the body becomes *najis* (impure), we should wash it and also wear *ṭāhir* (pure) clothes.[8]

Al-*Qiblah* — the Direction (of Ka bah) which a Muslim Faces at *Ṣalāt*

Al-Qiblah — the Direction (of Ka bah) which a Muslim Faces at *Ṣalāt*

Then stand facing the Ka`bah, the House renowned for the remembrance of Prophet Ibrahim (A.S.) the hero and champion of monotheism along with his son Prophet Islmā'īl (A.S.). These two, the father and the son of pure temperament, once built this House at Makkah for the worship of Allah, the One and the Unique.

Islam has declared this House as the very focal point of monotheism, and the Muslims have been ordered to turn their faces towards it, wherever in the world they may be, during the performance of their *ṣalāt* so that it becomes the focal centre of monotheism. The Holy Qur'ān says:

«وَمِنْ حَيْثُ خَرَجْتَ فَوَلِّ وَجْهَكَ شَطْرَ الْمَسْجِدِ الْحَرَامِ وَحَيْثُ مَا كُنْتُمْ فَوَلُّوا وُجُوهَكُمْ شَطْرَهُ...

"And from whatsoever place you set out, turn your face towards Al-Masjidu-Ḥarām (the Sacred Mosque); and wherever you are, turn your faces towards it..."

(The Holy Qur'ān, 2: 150)

The place where we perform *ṣalāt* and our dress should be unobjectionable, i.e., not having been acquired by force, nor by violation of the rights of others, nor these should be prohibited from other Islamic viewpoints.

How to perform the *Ṣalāt*

How to perform the *Ṣalāt*

At first we should condition our soul for worshipping the Almighty Allah. Then by expelling all other thoughts from our mind, we focus our entire attention towards Him.

Beginning with *Takbīr* after Resolving for *Ṣalāt* (Fig. 1)

In all sincerity and whole-heartedly we utter "*Allāhu Akbar*" i.e., Allah is the Greatest. Allah is Supreme and Sublime. Allah is incomprehensible and beyond our imagination.

Thus, with the utterance of *Allāhu Akbar*, the greatness of all other things vanishes from the eyes of the worshipper. He then thinks of nothing but the grandeur of Allah and with all his heart and soul, he stands humbly before his Creator for *ṣalāt* and glorification.

Standing Upright (Thinking Solely of Allah) (Fig. 2)

From this moment, until the end of the *ṣalāt*, ever facing the Ka'bah (Fig. 2), he keeps on addressing Allah lovingly and praisingly, refraining from speaking or replying to anyone around him.

Next in adoration and praise of Allah, we first read *Sūratul-Ḥamd*, paying careful attention to its valuable meaning.

بِسْمِ اللّٰهِ الرَّحْمٰنِ الرَّحِيمِ

Bismi-Llāhi-r-Raḥmāni-r-Raḥīm
(In the Name of Allah, the Beneficent, the Merciful.)

اَلْحَمْدُ لِلّٰهِ رَبِّ الْعٰالَمِينَ

Al-ḥamdu li-Llāhi Rabbi-l-ālamīn
(All praise is due to Allah, the Lord of the worlds.)

A Muslim begins every work and every speech with the Name of Allah. In the Islamic society, everything is begun with the Name of Allah Almighty.

In Islam, praise is due only to Allah, whose perfection is infinite. Besides Him none (nobody and nothing) is worthy of praise. One can express one's appreciation for someone or something, but within the limit of his or its worth. Thanks should be given in accordance with the service and kindness rendered. But appreciation and thanks must not take the form of flattery. Flattery and exaggerated praise is detrimental to morality and calamitous to society.

An exaggerating panegyrist and flatterer destroys his own personality and through his exaggerated eulogy and flattery, he debases himself. He further encourages people to project false images of themselves. These persons become increasingly more showy and self-conceited. They soon stop reflecting upon their own shortcomings to which they turn a blind eye, and show aversion to criticism of their behaviour by others.

Allowing themselves to become the victims of these mean flatterers, they become self-centred, obstinate, proud and dangerous idols, who consciously or unconsciously, expect all others to respect them even to the point of adoration. They expect blind acceptance of their thoughts and views and strict obedience to their orders.

Islam stresses constantly that:

"Praise is due only to Allah"

Thus, Islam sees to it that such pompous and arrogant "idols" do not appear in the monotheistic Islamic society, thereby ensuring impartial and logical criticism of anyone, irrespective of rank or position.

اَلرَّحْمٰنِ الرَّحِيمِ

Ar-Raḥmāni-r-Raḥīm.
(The Beneficent, the Merciful.)

مٰالِكِ يَوْمِ الدِّينِ

Māliki Yawmi-d-Dīn.
(The Master of the Day of Judgement.)

Although a Muslim believes in the mercy and forgiveness of Allah and is hopeful of His Compassion, yet on the other hand, as Allah is Just, he fears His punishment. He does not get self-conceited, and knows that his good and bad deeds will be weighed on the Day of Judgement.

اِيّٰاكَ نَعْبُدُ وَاِيّٰاكَ نَسْتَعِينَ

Iyyāka na'budu wa Iyyāka nasta'īn
(You (Alone) we worship and you (Alone) we ask for help.)

A Muslim always relies upon Allah and the abounding possibilities and power bestowed upon him by providence, and never extends his hand to any individual for help.

Of course he does accept the help of others in the performance of his task. But this help is either by way of contract or out of friendship and cordiality or as per the rules, and regulations, which are by themselves a kind of social contracts. However, in return for any help rendered, he pays for it in cash or credit through his dealings; neither others' help to him nor his help to others has any tint of pompous bossiness or charging obligation for favour done.

A Muslim neither accepts any aid with lordliness, nor does he look for help from anyone with expectation and greed.

He instead relies on Allah, and works hard, utilising his potentials and Allah-gifted faculties. He is happy with a moderate income which meets his daily needs, and leads an honest and pious life:

اِهْدِنَا الصِّرٰاطَ الْمُسْتَقِيمَ

Ihdina-ṣ-ṣirāṭa-l-mustaqīm
(Guide us to the straight path.)

صِراٰطَ الَّذِينَ اَنْعَمْتَ عَلَيْهِمْ

Sirata-lladhina an'amta `alayhim.
(The path of those whom you have favoured;

غَيْرِ الْمَغْضُوبِ عَلَيْهِمْ وَلاَ الضّاٰلّينَ

ghayri-l-maghḍūbi ‘alayhim wala-ḍḍāllīn
not [the path] of those who incur your wrath,
nor [of] those who go astray.)

This is the most basic prayer (supplication) and faithful devotion which every Muslim makes in his daily Ṣalawāt. Communing heartily with Allah, he prays to Him to keep him always on the right path in life; the path of those on whom He has been gracious and bountiful and he can benefit from it; not of those with whom He has been angry (due to their disobedience or carelessness), nor of those who go astray, and not to let his valuable potentials be wasted in wrong directions.

Meanwhile he prays to Allah to grant him his prayer.

The first sūrah (chapter) of Al-*Ḥamd* (the Opening of the Book) ends here.

After this *sūrah*, Al-*Ḥamd*, the worshipper recites any other surah from the Holy Qur'ān like surah 112, *"At-Tawḥīd"* (Monotheism) as follows:

بِسْمِ اللّٰهِ الرَّحْمٰنِ الرَّحِيمِ

Bismi-Llāhi-r-Raḥmāni-r-Raḥīm
(In the Name of Allah, the Beneficent, the Merciful.)

قُلْ هُوَاللّٰهُ اَحَدٌ

Qul Huwa-Llāhu Aḥad
(Say: He is Allah, the One.)

اَللّٰهُ الصَّمَدُ

Allāhu-ṣ-Ṣamad
(Allah is free from want, and eternally besought of all)

لَمْ يَلِدْ وَلَمْ يُولَدْ

Lam yalid wa lam yūlad
(He begets not, nor is He begotten.)

وَلَمْ يَكُنْ لَهُ كُفُوًا اَحَدٌ

Wa lam yakun lahū Kufuwan aḥad
(And there is none comparable unto Him.)

This is a Muslim's faith in Allah, which is against other superstitious beliefs. For instance, most Christians believe in the "Trinity", i.e., the combination of God, viz, a father, who has a son, and a third god, namely, the Holy spirit, Gabriel.

They combine these three into one and worship them in "Trinity of God". Also, they stand before the statue of Virgin Mary, the mother of Jesus, or other prominent religious figures for supplication and glorification.

Rukū' (Fig. 3)

After extolling Allah, praying to and imploring Him, the Muslim worshipper bows down touching the knees with his hands to honour His Magnificence, and in this posture of *rukū'* (genuflexion) he praises Allah and expresses love and sincere devotion to Him in the following words.

سُبْحَانَ رَبِّىَ الْعَظِيمِ وَبِحَمْدِهِ.

Ṣubḥāna Rabbiya-l-'Aẓimi wa bi-ḥamdih
(My Lord the Great is free from any imperfection; and praise be upon Him.)

Or, he says:

سُبْحَانَ اللّٰهِ، سُبْحَانَ اللّٰهِ، سُبْحَانَ اللّٰهِ

Subḥāna-Llāh, Ṣubḥāna-Llāh, Subḥāna-Llāh
(Allah is free from any imperfection.)

By uttering these words in this posture, the prayer-performer repeats the slogan of monotheism meaning to say:

"O Allah Almighty. The only Grandeur and Magnificence that makes me bow and bend down to the knees is Yours! I shall never bow and genuflect before anyone and anything in obeisance and homage except you. I shall keep my head upright in front of all natural and human powers, and shall never allow this free will and reason, and straight stature that you have given me, to genuflect before these powers."

This is how a Muslim, who treads the path of Islam feels and thinks. He keeps his head upright before all men of power, position, wealth and rank, and bends or bows before none.

He then lifts his head from this position, "*rukū*`" and stands upright.

Sujūd (Prostration) (Fig. 4)

And again, in the presence of this `Divine perfection', he touches the ground with his forehead for *sujūd*[9] submitting before His Magnificence in all humbleness and humility. He places the tips of the big toes of both feet, the knees, the palms and the forehead on the ground in *sujūd* and praises Allah saying:

سُبْحانَ رَبِّيَ الْاَعْلى وِبِحَمْدِهِ.

Subḥāna Rabbiya-l-'A`lā wa biḥamdih
(My Lord the Most High, is free from any imperfection; and praise be upon Him.)

Or, he says:

سُبْحانَ اللّهِ، سُبْحانَ اللّهِ، سُبْحانَ اللّهِ

Ṣubḥana-Llah, Subḥana-Llah, Subḥana-Llah
(Allah is free from any imperfection.)

Uttering these words, while still in *sujūd*, which is a sign of complete humility and submission, the worshipper once again repeats the spiritual tone of monotheism in his heart, meaning to say:

"Others prostrate for the wealthy and powerful beings other than Allah, but since I am a Muslim, I prostrate on the ground only for Allah, Who is the Greatest. And I shall never prostrate in the presence of anyone and anything except Him."

He then raises his head from the ground and sits upright at ease. Having done so, he once again prostrates, placing his forehead on the ground and repeating the above-mentioned words of glorification and praise of Allah. He then lifts his head off the ground and sits upright for *tashahhud* (saying the two testimonies), (Fig. 5)

The *Raka'āt* (Joined Units) of *Ṣalāt*

The *Raka'āt* (Joined Units) of *Ṣalāt*

From the time of reciting `*Sūratul-Ḥamd* until now, i.e. at the point of lifting the head off the ground, is called "one *rak'ah* of *Ṣalāt*", i.e. one related unit of *Ṣalāt*. This is because it includes one `*rukū'*'. Each of the daily ṣalawāt consists of either two, three or four *raka`at* (*rak'ahs*).

Ṣalātuṣ-Ṣubḥ is a two-*rak'ah ṣalāt*. *Ṣalātul-Maghrib* is of three raka`āt. *Ṣalātuẓ-Ẓuhr*, *ṣalātul'Aṣr*, and *ṣalātul-'Ishā'* are of four *raka'āt*, but while travelling these become two-rak`ah *ṣalāt* each.

For those who know little abut *ṣalāt*, in order to make it easy for them to learn, we explain here only the *wājib* (obligatory) portion of each of the daily ṣalawāt in detail (leaving now the desirable acts).

1- Ṣalātus-*Ṣubḥ* (Morning Prayer)

After *wuḍū'*, and other preliminaries (preparatory actions), with clean heart, away from any kind of dissimulation, affectation, etc., we stand up for *Ṣalāt* facing the "*Qiblah* (Makkah)" and say:

اَللّٰهُ اَكْبَرُ.

Allāhu Akbar.

And we recite *Sūratul-Ḥamd* as follows:

بِسْمِ اللهِ الرَّحْمٰنِ الرَّحِيمِ

اَلْـحَمْدُ لِلهِ رَبِّ الْعَالَمِينَ ٢ اَلرَّحْمٰنِ الرَّحِيمِ ٣ مَالِكِ يَوْمِ الدِّينِ ٤ اِيَّاكَ نَعْبُدُ وَاِيَّاكَ نَسْتَعِينُ ٥ اِهْدِنَا الصِّرَاطَ الْمُسْتَقِيمَ ٦ صِرَاطَ الَّذِينَ اَنْعَمْتَ عَلَيْهِمْ غَيْرِ الْمَغْضُوبِ عَلَيْهِمْ وَلاَ الضَّالِّينَ ٧

1- Bismi-Llāhi-r-Raḥmāni-r-Raḥīm
2- Al-ḥamdu li-Llāhi Rabbi—l-`ālamīn 3- Ar-Raḥmāni-r-Raḥīm. 4- Māliki Yawmi-d-Dīn. 5- Iyyāka na'budu wa Iyyāka nasta'īn 6- Ihdina-ṣ-ṣirāṭal-mustaqīm 7- Ṣirāṭa-lladhīna an'amta 'alayhim; ghayri-l-maghḍūbi 'alayhim wala-ḍḍāllīn.)

We then recite another surah from the Holy Qur'ān, such as "*At-Tawḥīd*".

بِسْمِ اللهِ الرَّحْمٰنِ الرَّحِيمِ

قُــلْ هُوَاللهُ اَحَدٌ ٢ اَللهُ الصَّمَدُ ٣ لَمْ يَلِدْ وَلَمْ يُولَـدْ وَلَمْ يَكُنْ لَهُ كُفُواً اَحَدٌ» ٤

Bismi-Llāhi-r-Raḥmāni-r-Raḥīm
(1- Qul Huwa-Llāhu Aḥad 2- Allāhu-ṣ-Ṣamad. 3- Lam yalid wa lam yūlad 4- Wa lam yakun lahu kufuwan aḥad.)

We then bow in humility and reverence for the Greatness of Allah, resting the palms upon the knees in *rukū'*. We glorify and praise Allah in this position saying:

سُبْحَانَ رَبِّيَ الْعَظِيمِ وَبِحَمْدِهِ

Subḥāna Rabbiya-l-`Aẓīmi wa bi-hamdih.

Or: سُبْحَانَ اللهِ، سُبْحَانَ اللهِ، سُبْحَانَ اللهِ

Subhana-Llāh, Subhana-Llāh, Subḥana-Llāh

We then stand upright, and go down to perform *sujūd* before Allah, the Most High. By placing on the ground the tips of the big toes, knees, and palms, and resting the forehead on the ground, stone, wood, mat or the like, we perform *sujūd*. Here again we glorify and praise Allah Almighty, Who is Greater than all, saying:

سُبْحَانَ رَبِّيَ الْأَعْلَىٰ وِبِحَمْدِهِ.

Subḥāna Rabbiya-l-'A`lā wa bi-ḥamdih.

Or:

سُبْحَانَ اللَّهِ، سُبْحَانَ اللَّهِ، سُبْحَانَ اللَّهِ.

Subḥāna-Llāh, Subḥāna-Llāh, Subḥāna-Llāh

We then lift the head and sit at ease.

Once again we perform *sujūd*, as explained before, placing the forehead on the ground saying:

سُبْحَانَ رَبِّيَ الْأَعْلَىٰ وِبِحَمْدِهِ.

Subḥāna Rabbiya-l-'A`lā wa bi-ḥamdih.

Or:

سُبْحَانَ اللَّهِ، سُبْحَانَ اللَّهِ، سُبْحَانَ اللَّهِ.

Subḥāna-Llāh, Subḥāna-Llāh, Subḥāna-Llāh

We then raise the head and sit at ease, with folded knees.

Thus, we complete one *rak`ah* of the two-*rak`ah* *Ṣalātus-Ṣubḥ*.

We then proceed with the second *rak`ah*. We get up and stand still. We recite "*Sūratul-Ḥamd*" and another surah such as "*At-Tawḥīd*" while standing. We then perform *rukū`*, and two sajdahs, as described earlier.

We then raise the head from the second *sajdah*, to complete the second *rak`ah*, sit with folded knees as in (Fig. 5) and recite:

اَشْهَدُ اَنْ لَا اِلٰهَ اِلَّا اللّٰهُ وَحْدَهُ لَا شَرِيكَ لَهُ.

Ashhadu an lā ilāha illa-Llāh, waḥdahu lā sharīka lah.

(I bear witness that there is no god but Allah; He is Alone, and to Him there is no partner.)

وَاَشْهَدُ اَنَّ مُحَمَّداً عَبْدُهُ وَرَسُولُهُ.

Wa ashhadu anna Muḥammadan `Abduhu wa Rasūluh.

(I bear witness that Muḥammad (S.A.) is His servant and His Messenger.)

اَللّٰهُمَّ صَلِّ عَلٰى مُحَمَّدٍ وَاٰلِ مُحَمَّدٍ.

Allāhumma ṣalli `alā Muḥammadin wa Āli Muḥammad

(O Allah, bless Muḥammad (S.A.) and his Descendants.)

اَلسَّلَامُ عَلَيْكَ اَيُّهَا النَّبِيُّ وَرَحْمَةُ اللّٰهِ وَبَرَكَاتُهُ.

As-salāmu `alayka ayyuha-n-Nabiyyu wa raḥmatu-Llāhi wa barakātuh.

(Peace, mercy and blessings of Allah be upon you O Prophet!)

اَلسَّلَامُ عَلَيْنَا وَعَلٰى عِبَادِ اللّٰهِ الصَّالِحِينَ.

As-salāmu `alayna wa `alā `ibādi-Llāhi-ṣ-ṣāliḥīn

(Peace be upon us and all Allah's righteous servants)

اَلسَّلَامُ عَلَيْكُمْ وَرَحْمَةُ اللّٰهِ وَبَرَكَاتُهُ.

As-salāmu alaykum wa raḥmatu-Llāhi wa barakātuh[10]

(Peace, mercy and blessings of Allah be upon you all.)

Thus, the *ṣalātus-subh* ends here.

In this last part of the *ṣalāt* once again the prayer-performer acknowledges the uniqueness of Allah and says clearly:

"Muḥammad (S.A.) is a servant and Messenger of Allah. And I pray to Allah to send His blessings to him, his descendants, and all other righteous believers."

Muslims utter this sentence: "Muḥammad (S.A.) is a servant of Allah," at least nine times a day. They do so to avoid going astray like the Christians who exalt Jesus from the position of servitude to Allah to the state of Divinity, or semi-Divinity, or call him the Son of Allah.

Muslims seek peace and blessings of Allah for the prophet (S.A.), the great leader of Islam, his infallible descendants, and the righteous. They declare that all Muslims, the righteous and pious believers, to whatever corner of the world they may belong, are from one Islamic *Ummah*. This attachment prevails so widely and deeply among them that even when a Muslim performs *ṣalāt* alone, he feels himself among his other Muslim brothers. Thus, at the end of each *ṣalāt*, he says *salām* (greetings) to them all, addressing them directly with these words "*As-salāmu 'alaykum wa raḥmatu-Llāhi wa barakātuh*" (Peace and Allah's mercy and blessings be upon you all.)

2. *Ṣalātuẓ-Ẓuhr* (Noon Prayer)

After *wuḍū'* and other preliminaries, with a clean heart, free from all dissimulation, affectation and pretence, we stand up facing the "*Qiblah*" with the *niyyah* (intention) for four *rak'ah*s and we say "*Allāhu Akbar*".

Rak ah 1

We then recite "*Sūratul-Ḥamd*" and follow it with another surah from the Holy Qur'ān such as "*At-Tawḥīd.*

We the perform *rukū'*, after which we rise and stand upright. We then perform *sujūd*, and then lift up the head and sit upright. We again perform *sujūd* after which we sit at ease with folded knees (Fig. 5)

Rak`ah 2

We then get up and stand upright to perform the second *rak'ah* of the *ṣalāt.*

Once again we recite "*Sūratul-Ḥamd*", and another surah from the Holy Qur'ān or the same surah of "*At-Tawḥīd*".

We then perform *rukū'*, after which we rise and stand upright. Having done so, we perform *sujūd.*

We then sit at ease (Fig. 5). This is followed by performing the second *sujūd* (*sajdah*) after which we sit at ease and say:

اَشْهَدُ أَنْ لا اِلٰهَ اِلاَّ اللهُ وَحْدَهُ لا شَرِيكَ لَهُ.

وَاَشْهَدُ اَنَّ مُحَمَّداً عَبْدُهُ وَرَسُوْلُهُ. اَللّٰهُمَّ صَلِّ عَلٰى مُحَمَّدٍ وَآلِ مُحَمَّدٍ.

"Ashhadu an lā ilāha illa-Llāh, waḥdahu lā sharīka lah. Wa ashhadu anna Muḥammadan 'Abduhu wa Rasūluh. Allāhumma ṣalli 'alā Muhammadin wa Āli Muhammad."

Rak`ah 3

We then stand up to perform the third *rak'ah* of the *ṣalāt.* To do so, we recite "*Sūratul-Hamd*", or instead say:

سُبْحَانَ اللهِ وَالْحَمْدُ لِلّٰهِ وَلَا اِلٰهَ اِلَّا اللهُ وَاللهُ اَكْبَرُ.

"Subḥāna-Llāhi wal-ḥamdu li-Llāhi wa lā ilāha illa-Llāhu wa-Llāhu Akbar."
(Allah is Transcendent and devoid of any imperfection; all praise is due to Allah; there is no god but Allah; and Allah is the Greatest).

After this we perform *rukūʻ* and then rise and stand upright. We then perform *sujūd*, and then raise the head and sit still. After this we again perform the second *sujūd*, and then stand up to perform the fourth *rakʻah*. Here, we once again recite "*Sūratul-Ḥamd*", or instead say:

سُبْحَانَ اللهِ وَالْحَمْدُ لِلّٰهِ وَلَا اِلٰهَ اِلَّا اللهُ وَاللهُ اَكْبَرُ.

"Subḥāna-Llāhi wal-ḥamdu li-Llāhi wa lā illāha illa-Llāhu wa-Llāhu Akbar."

After this, we perform *rukūʻ*, after which we stand upright. We then perform *sujūd*, raise the head from this position and sit still as in (Fig. 5). We perform *sujūd* once again, then raise the head and sit upright, and recite the *tashahhud* and *salām* successively as follows:

اَشْهَدُ اَنْ لَا اِلٰهَ اِلَّا اللهُ وَحْدَهُ لَا شَرِيكَ لَهُ.
وَاَشْهَدُ اَنَّ مُحَمَّداً عَبْدُهُ وَرَسُولُهُ. اَللّٰهُمَّ صَلِّ عَلٰى مُحَمَّدٍ وَّالِ مُحَمَّدٍ
اَلسَّلَامُ عَلَيْكَ اَيُّهَا النَّبِيُّ وَرَحْمَةُ اللهِ وَبَرَكَاتُهُ.
اَلسَّلَامُ عَلَيْنَا وَعَلٰى عِبَادِ اللهِ الصَّالِحِينَ. اَلسَّلَامُ عَلَيْكُمْ وَرَحْمَةُ اللهِ وَبَرَكَاتُهُ

"Ashhadu an lā ilāha illa-Llāh, waḥdahu lā sharīka lah. Wa ashhadu anna Muḥammadan ʻAbduhu wa Rasūluh. Allāhumma ṣalli ʻalā Muḥammadin wa Āli Muḥammad. As-salāmu ʻalaykum ayyuha-n-Nabiyyu wa rahmatu-Llāhi wa barakātuh. As-salāmu ʻalaynā wa ʻalā ʻibādi-Llāhi-

ṣṣāliḥīn. As-salāmu 'alaykum wa raḥmatu-Llāhi wa
barakātuh."

3. Ṣalātul- 'Aṣr (Afternoon Prayer)

This ṣalāt is performed exactly as Ṣalātuz-Zuhr.

4. Ṣalātul-Maghrib (After Sunset [Early Evening] Prayer)

Ṣalātul-Maghrib is of three raka 'āt (rak 'ahs). Therefore,
after raising the head from the second sujūd (sajdah) of
the third rak 'ah instead of getting up to perform the fourth
rak 'ah, we remain seated and recite tashahhud and end
with salām as follows:

اَشْهَدُ اَنْ لَا اِلٰهَ اِلَّا اللّٰهُ وَحْدَهُ لَا شَرِيكَ لَهُ.

وَاَشْهَدُ اَنَّ مُحَمَّداً عَبْدُهُ وَرَسُولُهُ.

اَللّٰهُمَّ صَلِّ عَلٰى مُحَمَّدٍ وَالِ مُحَمَّدٍ.

اَلسَّلَامُ عَلَيْكَ اَيُّهَا النَّبِىُّ وَرَحْمَةُ اللّٰهِ وَبَرَكَاتُهُ.

اَلسَّلَامُ عَلَيْنَا وَعَلٰى عِبَادِاللّٰهِ الصَّالِحِينَ.

اَلسَّلَامُ عَلَيْكُمْ وَرَحْمَةُ اللّٰهِ وَبَرَكَاتُهُ.

"Ashhadu an lā ilāha illa-Llāh, waḥdahu lā sharīka lah.
Wa ashhadu anna Muḥammadan 'Abduhu wa Rasūluh.
Allāhumma ṣalli 'alā Muḥammadin wa Āli Muḥammad.
As-salāmu 'alayka ayyuha-n-Nabiyyu wa raḥmatu-Llāhi
wa barakātuh. As-salāmu 'alaynā wa 'alā 'ibādi-Llāhi-
ṣṣāliḥīn. As-salāmu 'alaykum wa raḥmatu-Llāhi wa
barakātuh."

5- Ṣalātul- 'Ishā' (Dusk or [Early Night] Prayer)

This ṣalāt is performed exactly as the Ṣalātuz-Zuhr.[11]

Ṣalāt Deep Influence on Man

Ṣalāt Deep Influence on Man

The *ṣalāt* (Islamic prayer) can be called as follows:

"The hymn of monotheism and worshipping of the only one God, Allah."

"The hymn which protects man's personality."

"The hymn of purity and virtue."

"The hymn of peace and good relations with all the righteous men of Allah."

It is the hymn which all Muslims must recite five times daily, so that remembrance of and faith in Allah become stronger, enabling man to sustain and keep alive his high human qualities and guard against the deviation from the right Divine path. It guards him too, against the pollution of attributing associates to Allah Almighty, getting morally corrupt by the influence of enticing beauties or worldly pleasures, fear of the self-centred powers, and disagreement with Allah's righteous servants. It also safeguards him from all other spiritual corruptions.

It is like the hymn (that) the soldiers recite every morning and evening, to keep the spirit of heroism and courage alive, or like the hymn the pioneers recite to strengthen their spirit of benevolence and beneficence.

The following Qur'ānic verse reflects the profound influence of the "Ṣalāt" on the personality of man.

اُتْلُ مَا اُوْحِیَ اِلَیْكَ مِنَ الْكِتَابِ وَ اَقِمِ الصَّلٰوۃَ اِنَّ الصَّلٰوۃَ تَنْهٰی عَنِ الْفَحْشَاءِ وَالْمُنْكَرِ وَلَذِكْرُ اللّٰهِ اَكْبَرُ وَاللّٰهُ یَعْلَمُ مَا تَصْنَعُوْنَ.

"Recite that which has been revealed to you of the Book, and keep up the ṣalāt. Surely, the ṣalāt keeps (one) away from indecency and evil, and certainly remembrance, of Allah is the greatest, and Allah knows what you do."
(The Holy Qur'ān 29: 45)

Ṣalāt brings man spiritual felicity and prevents his soul from getting dull, sad, and despondent.

Ṣalāt is an action which develops the sense of duty and responsibility. A committed man who makes a point of performing ṣalawāt (prayers) regularly, cultivates a commendable habit, and at least respects one moral obligation and Islamic duty. This habit discourages carelessness and negligence on his part towards other duties. It makes him a useful person and helps him to progress in the course of his life. The Holy Qur'ān says:

وَاسْتَعِیْنُوْا بِالصَّبْرِ وَالصَّلٰوۃِ وَاِنَّهَا لَكَبِیْرَۃٌ اِلَّا عَلَی الْخَاشِعِیْنَ. اَلَّذِیْنَ یَظُنُّوْنَ اَنَّهُمْ مُلَاقُوْا رَبِّهِمْ وَاَنَّهُمْ اِلَیْهِ رَاجِعُوْنَ.

"And seek help through patience and ṣalāt, and truly it is hard except for the humble-minded,

who know that they shall meet their Lord, and that they shall return to Him."

(The Holy Qur'ān, 2: 45-46)

Ṣalāt to some people seems to be a burdensome duty. But to those, who have faith in the eternal life (of the Hereafter) and believe that they should always keep themselves pure, virtuous and away from evil, and strive towards becoming a relatively perfect being so that they may return to Allah, the All-Perfect, the Almighty, the Merciful, is always an exhilarating, delightful and pleasant experience.

Islam right from its early days, has invited Muslims to perform *ṣalawāt* (prayers). In the beginning, when none other than the prophet (S.A.), his wife Khadijah, and his cousin (uncle's son), 'Alī (A.S.) had embraced Islam, the prophet (S.A.) and 'Alī (A.S.) used to go to the valleys around Makkah to perform *ṣalāt.*[12]

Those who opposed Islam used to ridicule the prayer-performers and sometimes, even attack and harm them. To perform their *ṣalāt* in peace, the Muslims used to go to the valleys around Makkah and perform their *ṣalāt* there in congregation. But the opponents often used to obstruct them, and occasionally, clashes also occurred.[13]

The pressure, harm and ridicule from antagonists, instead of discouraging the Muslims from performing their obligatory *ṣalawāt,* rather served to increase their pleasure in performing this pleasing duty of worshipping Allah.

Prophet Muḥammad (S.A.) had told them that *ṣalāt* is the main slogan of monotheism and that Muslims should never neglect it.

Banū Thaqīf, was one of the great tribes which settled in the city of Ṭa'īf and its suburbs. In the eighth year of Hijrah, i.e., about three years before the passing away of prophet Muḥammad (S.A.), Banū Thaqīf sent some delegates to Madinah to discuss about their conversion to Islam, on certain conditions.

These delegates informed the Holy prophet (S.A.) that the Banū Thaqīf tribe would set forth a proposal for accepting Islam that they be exempted from performing the *ṣalawāt* (prayers).

The Prophet (S.A.) answered:

"...Insofar as *ṣalāt* is concerned, if the conversion to Islam is not accompanied by performing the *ṣalawāt*, then this conversion is of no value...."[14]

If a Muslim finds himself in a situation where he is unable to perform his *ṣalāt* in a normal way, he should then do so in whatever way he is able to do in that particular situation like: sitting, lying on bed, riding on a horse, in a car, train or a plane, or sitting behind a tank or any other armoured vehicle, etc.

Ṣalātul-Jamā'ah
(Congregational Prayer)

Ṣalātul-Jamā'ah (Congregational Prayer)

Islam emphasises that Muslims should lead a community life, and even perform the *ṣalāt* in congregation. If there is a mosque, they should perform *ṣalāt* there. Otherwise, they should gather at a suitable place, such as a desert, a school-hall, a workshop, a factory, or a house.

In case there is place where *ṣalātul-jamā'ah* is performed, then everyone should try to leave his home or office and join other Muslim brothers there to perform the *ṣalāt* together.

In *ṣalātul-jamā'ah,* the prayer-performers stand up in orderly rows, all facing the *Qiblah.* One person stands up ahead to lead the *ṣalāt,* and he is called the "*imām*" (leader) of the *ṣalātul-jamā'ah.*

Ṣalātul-jamā'ah is normally led by the highest ranking representative of the Islamic government in each region. Or else, people select from among themselves a proper and worthy person to lead the *ṣalāt.*

In *ṣalātul-jamā'ah*, *Sūratul-Ḥamd* and another surah like *At-Tawḥīd* in the first and second *rak'ah*s are recited by the *imām* only, while the other prayer-performers remain silent and just listen. But in the remaining *raka'āt,* all the other prayer phrases are recited together by all.

Ṣalātul-Jumu‘ah
(Friday Prayer)

Ṣalātul-Jumu'ah (Friday Prayer)

On Friday noon, the Muslims from different areas (within a radius of about six kilometres) assemble and perform *Ṣalātul-Jumu'ah*. In this *ṣalāt*, the *imām*, of the *Jamā'ah* first stands up facing the audience and begins his speech by praising and thanking Allah, and by reciting verses from the Holy Qur'ān and Hadith. He recites and explains at least one surah from the Holy Qur'ān. He talks about the teachings of Islam, and discusses the socio-political problems of the Islamic *Ummah*, in two sermons (*Khuṭbahs*). At the end of the second *khuṭbah*, everybody stands up together to perform "two-*rak'ah*" *Ṣalātul-Jumu'ah* which is similar to *Ṣalātul-Subh*.

In fact, the two *Khuṭbahs* delivered, before the beginning of the *ṣalāt*, are counted as two *rak'ah*s of *ṣalāt*.

Wherever, a just statesman rules in a dominion, the *Ṣalātul-Jumu'ah* must be held. Wherever his representative is present, he himself must personally take the responsibility of leading *Ṣalātul-Jumu'ah*. If he cannot do so, he must appoint someone else in his place.

And as soon as the *Adhān* of *Ṣalātul-Jumu'ah* is heard, all Muslims must stop working and come to the place where the *ṣalāt* is being held.

يَا أَيُّهَا الَّذِينَ آمَنُوا إِذَا نُودِىَ لِلصَّلٰوةِ مِنْ يَوْمِ الْجُمُعَةِ فَاسْعَوْا إِلَىٰ ذِكْرِ اللّٰهِ وَذَرُوا الْبَيْعَ ذٰلِكُمْ خَيْرٌ لَكُمْ إِنْ كُنْتُمْ تَعْلَمُونَ.

"O you who believe! When the call is heard for the ṣalāt on Friday, then hasten to the remembrance of Allah and leave off trading. That is better for you, if you know."

(The Holy Qur'ān 62:9)

Once the *ṣalāt* is over, everybody can leave and resume his work.

The Holy Qur'ān says:

فَإِذَا قُضِيَتِ الصَّلٰوةُ فَانْتَشِرُوا فِى الْأَرْضِ وَابْتَغُوا مِنْ فَضْلِ اللّٰهِ وَاذْكُرُوا اللّٰهَ كَثِيراً لَعَلَّكُمْ تُفْلِحُونَ.

"And when the prayer (ṣalāt) is ended, then disperse in the land and seek of Allah's grace, and remember Allah much, that you may be successful."

The Holy Qur'ān 62: 10)

If the government is not headed by a just man, or if a Muslim community is settled in a certain place where a representative of the government of the just Imam is absent, it is better that a just and qualified person be chosen from among them who can deliver two khuṭbahs (sermons) before the *ṣalāt*, and lead *Ṣalātul-Jumu'ah*. Otherwise, they can perform *Ṣalātuẓ-Ẓuhr* as usual.

The first *Ṣalātul-Jumu'ah* after Hijrah

When the Holy Prophet (S.A.) emigrated from Makkah to Madinah, he stopped in its suburb at a place called

"*Qubā*", where a small tribe of Arabs resided: A group of Muslims from different corners of the city came to see and welcome the Prophet (S.A.), while some others who were not residents of the city also joined them.

The Prophet (S.A.) stayed in "*Qubā*" from Sunday to Thursday, the period during which he constructed a small mosque which is known as "Masjid *Qubā*".

This was the first Islamic mosque which was built by the Muslims.[15]

On Friday Morning, the Prophet (S.A.) left Quba for the city, along with other Muslims. At noon they reached a valley where another small tribe of Arabs lived. Here, the Prophet (S.A) performed *Ṣalātul-Jumu'ah.* He first went ahead and stood before the ranks of Muslims present there and spoke to them about Islam, and about their duties during those early days of founding the Islamic government which they were expected to shoulder, in two sermons (*khuṭbahs*). Then he led them in congregation to perform together the two-*rak'ah Ṣalātul-Jumu'ah.*

Ṣalātul-'Īd (The Two-'Īd prayers — *'Īdul-Fiṭr* and *Al'Aḍḥā*)

Ṣalātul-'Īd (The Two-'Īd Prayers — *'Īdul-Fiṭr* and *Al-'Aḍḥā*)

In Islam, there are two formal festivals: "*'Īdul-Fiṭr*" and "*'Īdul-Qurbān*" or "*'Īdul-'Aḍḥā*".

'Īdul-Fiṭr, is celebrated at the end of fasting at the close of the *Ramaḍān* month, on the first of the lunar month *"Shawwāl"*. Muslims, after fasting throughout the month of Ramaḍān, break their fast on this day and having successfully completed this sacred worship, celebrate this festival together.

'Īdul-'Aḍḥā is celebrated on the tenth of the lunar month, *Dhul-Ḥijjah* when the main part of the *ḥajj* rituals has been performed by the Muslims, who go to Makkah to perform *ḥajj*. On this day, the Muslims sacrifice a sheep, a cow, or a camel, a part of which they eat themselves and the remaining meat is distributed to the needy.

Throughout the world Muslims celebrate this day, because of the completion of the main part of the magnificent *ḥajj* rituals.

These two great Festivals of Islam are the festivals of action and deed. During the *'Īdul-Fiṭr* festival, Muslims enjoy the feast for having successfully completed their fasting throughout the month of Ramaḍān. During the festival of *'Īdul-'Aḍḥā*, they celebrate the achievement of the Islamic *Ummah* for performing the magnificent rituals of *ḥajj*.

To celebrate these two annual Islamic festivals, Muslims from every corner of the city or town gather together in a area such as a square, a field or an open area of a desert, or a large hall if weather conditions do not permit an open-air gathering. They then joyfully say together "*Allāhu Akbar*", and praise Allah.

After this, they start glorifying Allah and perform the two-*rak'ah ṣalāt* in congregation.

At the end of the *ṣalāt*, the prayer-performers altogether say loudly "*Allāhu Akbar*" several times. And then the *imām* stands up facing the worshippers, and delivers two *khuṭbah*s (sermons).

Usually after the *ṣalāt*, the worshippers are offered some light refreshment.

Ṣalātul-Jumu'ah and *Ṣalātul-'Īd* are not only congregational prayers, but also a symbol of Islamic, social and political unity. Therefore, the responsibility to hold such congregations is among the prime duties of the Islamic government.

In places where the ruling government is other than an Islamic one, the Muslims must themselves take the necessary initiatives to establish these pure and valuable Islamic congregations for the worship and adoration of Allah, the One, the Unique.

Ṣalātul-jamā'ah, *Ṣalātul-Jumu'ah*, and *Ṣalātul-'Īd*, not only deeply affect the prayer-performers intellectually and help them in their spiritual growth, but also strengthen the brotherly feelings among them and enhance their unity and solidarity. These congregational *ṣalawāt* (prayers) are valuable Islamic symbols that must be carefully guarded and observed.

Ṣalātul-’Āyāt (The Prayer of Signs of the Divine power)

Ṣalātul-'Āyāt (The prayer of Signs of the Divine Power)

There are people who get terribly frightened and sometimes faint because of witnessing natural phenomena like the eclipse of the sun (*al-Kusūf*) or of the moon (*al-Khusūf*) [i.e. the interception or obscuration, complete or in part, of the sun's light or of the moon's light by another celestial body.], earthquakes, typhoons, thunderbolts, storms, thunders, lightnings, floods, and other frightful natural occurrences.

In Islam these occurrences, like thousands of other natural phenomena are visible signs of the splendid system of the universe created by the Almighty Allah. Therefore, these are the signs (*āyāt*) which manifest the wisdom and power of Allah Almighty.

Mankind must ponder deeply over these happenings and should not abondon themselves to mere fancy or imagination.

So at the time of a lunar or a solar eclipse, one should not undertake superstitious actions or follow the illusive and fanciful beliefs, which are customary among many superstitious tribes and nations,[16] but he should deeply think of Allah, direct his heart towards Him, and perform two-*rak'ah ṣalāt*, and thus rid himself of the superstitious thoughts which may result when he witnesses such happenings.

When there are earthquakes, typhoons, thunderbolts, thunders, lightnings, storms, floods and similar occurrences, which cause general fear and panic, one should only think of Allàh and realise that He has gifted man with the means to save himself from such natural disasters, and thereby escape their fearful consequences. One must find ways and use the means at one's disposal to save oneself and others from these calamities, so at the first opportunity, one must perform the two-*rak'ah ṣalāt*, praise and thank Allah, ask him for more and more blessings and mercy, and by such communing with Allah, he can attain tranquillity and peace of mind.

The two-*rak'ah Ṣalātul-'Āyāt* is like *Ṣalātuṣ-Ṣubḥ*. The only difference is that in each *rak'ah* of *ṣalāt*, instead of one *rukū'*, we have five. And in between every two *rukū*'s, we recite *Sūratul-Ḥamd* and another surah from the Holy Qur'ān. The surah which is recited after *Sūratul-Ḥamd* can also be divided into five parts. We recite the first part and then perform *rukū'* and continue reciting each part thereafter between every two *rukū*'s until we finish all the five parts of the *sūrah*. Therefore, we must choose a sūrah which contains five or more than five verses. For example, *Sūrat al-Kāfirūn* (the Disbelievers) i.e. Surah 109.

Ṣalātul-'Āyāt in its short form is performed as follows:

We first say "*Allāhu Akbar*", then recite *Sūratul-Ḥamd*, and then say:

بِسْمِ اللهِ الرَّحْمٰنِ الرَّحِيمِ.

Bismi-Llāhi-r-Raḥmāni-r-Raḥīm

(In the Name of Allah, the Beneficent the Merciful)

قُلْ يٰا اَيُّهَا الْكافِرُونَ.

Qul yā ayyuhal-Kāfirūn.
(Say: O disbelievers!)

We then perform the first *rukū'*, raise the head after it, stand upright and say:

لا اَعْبُدُ ما تَعْبُدُونَ.

Lā a`budu mā ta`budūn.
(I do not worship that which you worship.

We then perform *rukū'* a second time, after which we raise the head, stand upright and say:

وَلا اَنْتُمْ عابِدُونَ ما اَعْبُدُ.

Wa lā antum `ābidūna mā a`bud.
(Nor do you worship Him Whom I worship.)

We again perform *rukū'* for a third time, after which we raise the head again, stand upright and say:

وَلا اَنَا عابِدٌ ما عَبَدْتُمْ.
وَلا اَنْتُمْ عابِدُونَ ما اَعْبُدُ.

Wa lā anā `ābidun mā `abadtum.
Wa lā antum `ābidūna mā a`bud.
(And I shall not worship that which you worship.
Nor will you worship Him Whom I worship.)

We then perform the fourth *rukū'*, raise the head, stand upright and say.

Lakum dīnukum wa liya Dīn.
(For you is your religion and for me is my religion.)

(The Holy Qur'ān, 109: 1-6)

We then perform the fifth *rukū'*, raise the head, stand upright and perform *sujūd* twice on the ground.

After the second *sujūd*, we perform another *rak'ah* in the same manner, and then end the *ṣalāt* after reciting the *tashahhud* and *salām*.

Du'ā' Al-Qunūt (Supplication)

What ever has been said so far is of the *wājib* (obligatory) actions and recitations in the *ṣalāt*.

Besides this, one can commune with Allah in his *ṣalawāt* (prayers) the way he likes; he certainly wishes to tell Allah about his sorrows and desires, and express love and devotion to Him.

This kind of supplication is very good, desirable, and recommended especially in the second *rak'ah* of *ṣalāt* before *rukū'*. And if one forgets to recite it before the *rukū'* he can do it right after *rukū'*, and it is called "*qunūtuṣ-Ṣalāt*". Everybody can commune with Allah reciting *qunūt* (as shown in Fig. 6), express love and devotion to Him and tell Him about his needs and wishes in any form or wording he chooses.

Ṣalāt in the Language of the Holy Qur'ān

Ṣalāt in the Language of the Holy Qur'ān

From the very beginning of Islam, the Muslims have recited "*adhān* and *iqāmah*" (the calls for *ṣalāt*) and the *wājib* parts of the *ṣalāt* in Arabic which is the language of the Holy Qur'ān. Taking into consideration the fact that *ṣalāt* is very vital and is the great slogan of Islam and the Islamic *Ummah*, the Muslims of the world should consider themselves as a single, solid entity and a single *Ummah*. The common aspects and means of communication are necessary for the unity and solidarity of an *Ummah*. The Muslims organise the grand congregational *ṣalāt*, *Ṣalātul-Jumu'ah*, and the *ṣalāt* of *'Īdul-'Aḍḥā* during the *ḥajj* rituals at Makkah every year where hundreds of thousands of Muslims, whose languages are different, gather together from different corners of the world. The essential parts of *ṣalāt*, and *adhān* and *iqāmah* which are the calls for *ṣalāt* to the public, should better be in one common Islamic language so that everybody can understand it. And this common Islamic language should obvisouly be the language of the Holy Qur'ān, namely Arabic.

The *ṣalāt*, *adhān* and *iqāmah* are recited in 29 short Arabic sentences.

Learning these 29 Arabic sentences along with their clear meaning is easy for anybody who is interested.

At present in the advanced countries, one's cognition of a foreign language is considered a part of the general knowledge. A great number of people in these countries speak at least one foreign language.

And. this knowledge is regarded as a sign of the growth and advancement of every nation.

Therefore, the fact that the Muslims are duty-bound to learn the original wording of *ṣalāt* in Arabic is in itself a motivation for raising the level of general knowledge of Muslims.

So, in the next pages we are going to repeat, one after another, the 29 sentences with their short translations to make their memorisation by heart easier.

The Expressive Sentences of the *Adhān*, *Iqāmah*, and *Ṣalāt*

The Expressive Sentences of the *Adhān*, *Iqāmah*, and *Ṣalāt*

A. For *Adhān* and *Iqāmah*

Allāhu Akbar
(Allah is the Greatest.)

اَشْهَدُ اَنْ لاَ اِلٰهَ اِلاَّ اللّٰهُ.

Ashhadu an lā ilāha illa-Llāh
(I clearly observe and bear witness that there is no god, but Allah [the creator of the universe].)

اَشْهَدُ اَنَّ مُحَمَّداً رَسُولُ اللّٰهِ.

Ashhadu anna Muḥammadan Rasūlu-Llāh
(I clearly observe and bear witness that Muḥammad (S.A.) is the Messenger of Allah)

حَيَّ عَلَى الصَّلاٰةِ.

Ḥayya 'alaṣ-ṣalāh
(Hurry up to ṣalāt)

Ḥayya 'alal-falāḥ
(Hurry up to the deliverance.)

حَيَّ عَلٰى خَيْرِالْعَمَل.

Ḥayya 'alā Khayril-'amal
(Hurry up to the best deed.)

قَدْ قَامَتِ الصَّلٰاةُ.

Qad qāmatiṣ-ṣalāh
(Indeed *ṣalāt* has started)

اَللّٰهُ اَكْبَرُ.

Allāhu Akbar
(Allah is the Greatest)

لاٰ اِلٰهَ اِلاّٰ اللّٰهُ.

Lā ilāha illa-Llāh
(There is no god, but Allah.)

B. For *Ṣalāt* (Prayer)

اَللّٰهُ اَكْبَرُ.

Allāhu Akbar
(Allah is the Greatest)

بِسْمِ اللّٰهِ الرَّحْمٰنِ الرَّحِيمِ

Bismi-Llāhi-r-Raḥmāni-r-Raḥīm
(In the Name of Allah, the Beneficent, the Merciful.)

اَلْحَمْدُ لِلّٰهِ رَبِّ الْعَالَمِينَ

Al-Hamdu li-Llāhi Rabi-l-`ālamīn

(All praise is due to Allah, the Lord of the worlds)

اَلرَّحْمٰنِ الرَّحِيمِ

Ar-Raḥmānī-r-Raḥī
(The Beneficent, the Merciful)

مٰالِكِ يَوْمِ الدِّينِ

Māliki Yawmi-d-Dīn
The Master of the Day of Judgment

اِيّٰاكَ نَعْبُدُ وَاِيّٰاكَ نَسْتَعِينُ

Iyyāka na'budu wa Iyyāka nasta'īn
(You (alone) we worship and You (alone) we ask for help.)

اِهْدِنَا الصِّرٰاطَ الْمُسْتَقِيمَ

Ihdina-ṣ-ṣirāṭal-mustaqīm
(Guide us to the straight path)

صِرٰاطَ الَّذينَ اَنْعَمْتَ عَلَيْهِمْ

Ṣirāṭa-lladhīna an'amta 'alayhim
(The path of those whom You have favoured;)

غَيْرِ الْمَغْضُوبِ عَلَيْهِمْ

Ghayril-maghḍūbi `alayhim
(Not (the path) of those who incur Your wrath)

وَلاَ الضّٰالّينَ

Wa la-ḍḍāllīn
(Nor [of] those who go astray.)

بِسْمِ اللهِ الرَّحْمٰنِ الرَّحِيْمِ

Bismi-Llāhi-r-Raḥmāni-r-Raḥīm
(In the Name of Allah, the Beneficent, the Merciful.)

قُلْ هُوَاللّٰهُ اَحَدٌ

Qul Huwa-Llāhu Aḥad
(Say: He is Allah, the Unique.)

اَللّٰهُ الصَّمَدُ

Allāhu-ṣ-Ṣamad
(Allah is free from want, and eternally besought of All.)

لَمْ يَلِدْ وَلَمْ يُولَدْ

Lam yalid wa lam yūlad
(He begets not, nor is He begotten.)

وَلَمْ يَكُنْ لَهُ كُفُوًا اَحَدٌ

Wa lam yakun lahu kufuwan aḥad
(And there is none comparable unto Him)

سُبْحَانَ رَبِّىَ الْعَظِيمِ وَ بِحَمْدِهِ.

Subḥāna Rabbiya-l-`Aẓīmi wa bi-ḥamdih
(My Great Lord is free from any imperfection, and praise be upon Him.)

سُبْحَانَ رَبِّىَ الْاَعْلٰى وَ بِحَمْدِهِ.

Subḥāna Rabbiya-l-'A`lā wa bi-ḥamdih
(My Lord, the Most High, is free from any imperfection; and praise be upon Him.)

سُبْحَانَ اللّٰهِ وَالْحَمْدُلِلّٰهِ وَلَا اِلٰهَ اِلَّا اللّٰهُ وَاللّٰهَ اَكْبَرُ.

Subḥāna-Llāhi wal-ḥamdu li-Llāhi wa lā ilāha illa-Llāhu wa-Llāhu Akbar.

(Allah is Transcendent and devoid of any imperfection; praise be to Allah; there is no got but Allah; and Allah is the Greatest.)

اَشْهَدُ اَنْ لَا اِلٰهَ اِلَّا اللّٰهُ وَحْدَهُ لَا شَرِيكَ لَهُ.

Ashhadu an lā ilāha illa-Llāh Waḥahu lā shrīka lah

(I bear witness that there is no god, but Allah — the One and Unique and to Him there is no partner.)

وَاَشْهَدُ اَنَّ مُحَمَّداً عَبْدُهُ وَرَسُولُهُ.

Wa ashhadu anna Muḥammadan ʿAbduhu wa Rasūluh.

(And I bear witness that Muḥammad (S.A.) is His servant and His Messenger.)

اَللّٰهُمَّ صَلِّ عَلٰى مُحَمَّدٍ وَاٰلِ مُحَمَّدٍ.

Allāhumma ṣalli ʿalā Muḥammadin wa āli Muḥammad

(O Allah bless Muḥammad, and his Descendants.)

اَلسَّلَامُ عَلَيْكَ اَيُّهَا النَّبِيُّ وَرَحْمَهُ اللّٰهِ وَبَرَكَاتُهُ

As-salāmu ʿalayka ayyuha-n-Nabiyyu wa raḥmatu-Llāhi wa barakātuh.

(O prophet! We wish peace, mercy and blessings of Allah be upon you.)

اَلسَّلَامُ عَلَيْنَا وَ عَلٰى عِبَادِاللّٰهِ الصَّالِحِينَ.

As-salāmu `alaynā wa `alā `ibādī-Llāhi-ṣ-ṣāliḥīn.
(Peace be upon us and all Allah's righteous servants.)

اَلسَّلَامُ عَلَيْكُمْ وَرَحْمَةُ اللّٰهِ وَبَرَكَاتُهُ.

As-salāmu 'alaykum wa raḥmatu-Llāhi wa barakātuh.
(Peace, Mercy and blessings of Allah be upon you all.

Glossary of Non-English (Islamic) Terms

Glossary of Non-English Islamic Terms

A

Al-'A`lā:	The Most High, the Most Exalted [an Attribute of Allah]
adā':	Performing the duty duly or in time
adhān:	The proclamation for prayers, generally announced by the mu'adhdhin from the minaret or tower of the mosque
Allah:	The Islamic Name for God, the Creator and the Lord of the Worlds
Allāhu-Akbar:	Allah is the Great
(A.S.):	short for `Alayhis-*salām*, meaning Peace be upon him", usually said for the infallible Imams or the prophets individually
ashhadu:	I bear witness, I testify, I declare (that)
`aṣr:	afternoon, the period between midday (noon) and sunset (evening)

āyah:	Allah's clear and significant sign or proof for His creatures, a Qur'ānic verse
Al-`Aẓīm:	the Great [an Attribute of Allah]

B

Banū Thaqīf:	a large Arab tribe which lives in Aṭ-Ṭā'if during the eight year of Hijrah. Refer to the story on page (67) of this book.
barakātuh: (pl. of baraka)	Allah's blessings
bāṭil:	invalid, incorrect

D

dhikr or *dhikru-Llāh:*	remembering Allah by uttering some words for glorifying Him, or doing so by heart.
Dhul-Ḥijjah:	an Islamic Arabic month, the last month of the Lunar Hijri year (between Dhul-Qi`dah and Muḥarram)
Dhul - Qi`dah:	an Islamic Arabic month before the last month of Dhul-Hijjah invocation; supplication, imploring for Allah's blessings and help; prayer

F

Fajr: dawn; the first appearance of light in the sky before the sun rises

al-Falāh: deliverance from Hell, attaining the status of entering paradise

Fiqh: jurisprudence of religion's precepts and teachings

G

ghusl: washing the whole polluted body ritually; obligatory ritual bathing, which is required for certain types of uncleanliness

H

ḥayḍ: menstruation (monthly period) during which a mature female (woman) should abstain from performing obligatory prayers, fasting and some other obligatory religious duties; menstrual [monthly] discharge of a hot red blood from a woman's womb.

ḥajj: pilgrimage to Mecca, that must be made, at least once in life, by every Muslim who can afford it.

ḥamd: praising of Allah, renerding thanks to Allah

al-Hijjrah: the migration of Prophet Muḥammad (S.A.), from Mecca to Madinah, which marks the beginning of the Islamic Hijri calendar. It begins (on July 16th 622 A.D.)

I

'ibādah (*ibādatu-Llāh*): Divine worship; adoration of Allah; obedience and servitude to Almighty Allah; pious and faithful deeds evoted to Allah

'īd: feast, festival

'Īdul-'Aḍḥā (*'Īdul-Qurbān*): Festival day on the tenth of the month of Dhul-Ḥijjah

'Īdul-Fiṭr: Festival day on the first of the month of Shawwāl celebrating the end of the Ramaḍān fasting

imām: a religious leader; a leader of a religious group dealing with religious matters or affairs

imāmul-jamā'ah: a congregational prayer leader

imāmul-jumu'ah: an *imām* who leads the Friday prayers (*Ṣalātul-Jumu'ah*)

istiḥāḍah. excessive or (extraordinary) discharge of a yellowish cold blood after the usual menstruation (of a mature female [woman]), or at any undue time, whether little, fair or much.

al-iqāmah: the recitation (of the same *adhān* phrases with little difference) directly before starting the *ṣalāt* as a call for mental preparedness (towards Allah Almighty) with the intent to pray.

J

jamā`ah: c
ongregation, assembly

Al-Jumu'ah: Friday, the name of the last day of the week in the Islamic calendar

K

Ka`bah: t
he sanctuary oblong stone building, which is also called Al-Baytul-*Ḥarām*, the inviolable sacred House of the Almighty Allah in Makkah, built by prophet Ibrāhīm (A.S.) and his son Ismā'īl (A.S.) for worshipping Allah, the One and the Unique. It is also

considered concourse of people from all over the Islamic world. It is considered too, an important centre for all Muslims' worship, and hence they turn their face towards it in prayers.

al-Kāfirūn also *al-Kuffār* (pl. of *al-Kāfir*): the disbelievers; unbelievers; those who reject the belief in Allah Almighty and His Religion

Khayrul-`amal: the best of deeds which is the *ṣalāt* (performing prayers to Almighty Allah)

al-Khusūf (khusūful-qamar): the eclipse of the moon, that is, the interception or obscuration, complete or in part, of the moon's light by the intervention of another celestial body.

Khuṭbah: a sermon, especially in Friday - Prayer; a religious or/and political speech; an address.

al-Kusūf (kusūfush-Shams): the eclipse of the sun, that is, the interception or obscuration, complete or in part of the sun's light by the intervention of another celestial body.

M

Al-*Madīnah* or *Madīnah*: an important city in Arabia; it is also called *Madīnatun-Nabī* (the city of the

	Prophet Muḥammad [S.A.]); also called *Al-Madīnatul-Munawwarah*
Makkah (Mecca):	an important city in Arabia, and a great Islamic centre where all the Muslims of the world come to visit it for performing *ḥajj* pilgrimage, and it includes Ka`bah and Al-Baytul-Ḥarām, the sacred House of Allah Almighty. It is also the city where the prophet Muḥammad (S.A.) was born.
Mu'adhdhin:	a person who announces the *adhān* aloud calling people for *ṣalāt*
mustaḥabb:	desirable, commendable

N

najāsah (pl: *najāsāt*):	impurity, uncleanliness
najis:	(adj) impure, unclean
nifās:	the condition of discharging (of) blood of a woman after childbirth or abortion
niyyah:	intention (it is held in mind before starting the main *ṣalāt*

Q

qadā:	performing the due duty at later time

al-qiblah:	the direction of Ka`bah which a Muslim faces at prayer
qiyām:	the upright standing in *ṣalāt*, upright standing posture in prayers.
Qubā:	name of a place in the suburb of Madinah
qunūt:	raising the hands for supplication (*du'ā'*) during *ṣalāt*, especially after reciting the two surahs in the second *rak'ah*
Al-Qur'ānul-Majīd or Al-Qur'ānul-Karīm:	The Glorious Qur'ān or the Holy Qur'ān which is the Holy Book of Islam revealed by the Almighty Allah to the Holy Prophet Muḥammad (S.A.) of Islam — as the last and most perfect Divine Book for the whole humanity.

R

Rabbul-`ālamīn:	Lord of the worlds
Rabbī:	my Lord (Allah)
raḥmah:	mercy, willingness to forgive, not to punish; showing of kindness and sympathy to someone
raḥmatullāh:	mercy of Allah
rukū':	genuflexion or kneeling down in obedience and reverence to Allah Almighty

rak'ah (pl: *raka`āt*):	a unit of prayer (*ṣalāt*) consisting of three main postures standing, genuflexion and prostration (all with recitation)
Ramaḍān:	the ninth month of the lunar *Hijrī* year; the holy Islamic month during which ritual fasting is observed
Ar-riṣālatul-amaliyyah:	a treatise on the Islamic ritual practices for Muslims.
Rukū':	genuflexion; bowing down to the Almighty Allah in humility and reverence at prayer, in such a way that the palms of the hands touch the knees.

S

(S.A.):	Short for "*sallā-Llāhu `alayhi wa Alihi wa sallam*" i.e. Allah's peace and blessings be upon him and his descendants.
sijdah (pl: *sijdāt* or *sijdahs*):	an act of prostration in the *ṣalāt* or worship to Allah
salām:	general Islamic greeting
ṣalāt:	Arabic name for prayer
aṣ-ṣalātul-yawmiyyah:	any of the five ritual daily prayers

ṣalawāt:	plural of *ṣalāt* [prayer]; Arabic word used for greeting and wishing blessings and peace to Prophet Muḥammad (S.A.) and his Household and descendants.
Shawwāl:	the tenth month of the lunar *Hijrī* year, beginning with the break of the fast of Ramaḍān
Shī`ah:	Shi`ites; Muslim followers of the Prophet Muḥammad (S.A.) and his Household, the twelve infallible Imams (Imam `Alī and his (11) sons [A.S.]) consecutively
Shī'ī fiqh:	Islamic jurisprudence of the Shi`ah sect
ṣubḥ:	early morning
sujūd:	state or act of prostration; touching the ground with the forehead, palms, kness and two big tiptoes
sūrah:	a chapter of the Qur'ān which has a number of verses (*āyāhs*)
Sūratul-Ḥamd:	the first chapter of the Holy Qur'ān. It is also named "*Al-Fātiḥah*" (The Opening) or "*Fatiḥatul-Kitāb*" (The Opening of the Book), or "*Ummul-Qur'ān* (The Essence of the Qur'ān). It is recited twice in every daily prayer of the Muslims. It is an essential part of all Muslim worship, in congregation or alone.

Sūratut-Tawḥīd:	the Qur'ānic chapter (*sūrah*) of *At-Tawḥīd* (Monotheism). It has also been called "the essence of the Qur'ān". It was revealed to concisely show the Essence, Onencess and Uniqueness of the Almighty Allah. It is named too, "*Al-'Ikhlāṣ*" (Faithful worship and Loyalty to only Allah Almighty).

T

ta`ālim* (pl. of *ta`līm):	teachings, learnings
ṭāhir:	Islamically clean or pure
takbīr:	saying "*Allāhu Akbar*" (i.e., Allah is Great)
taqwā:	God-fearing and piety
tartīb:	the order or sequence as prescribed by the Islamic Shari`ah
tasbīḥ:	uttering the phrases for *dhikru-Llāh* like "*Subḥana-Llāh*", "*Al-Ḥamdu-lil-lāh*" "*Allāhu-Akbar*", etc.
tashahhud:	testifying to the Unity or Oneness of Allah, and Prophethood of Muḥammad (S.A.)
tayammum:	a ritual substitute for *wuḍū'* and *ghusl*, when for specific reasons, these acts are not possible.

tathlīth:	Trinity, in the Christian religion, the union of the 3 forms of God (the Father, son and Holy Spirit) as one God
Tawḥīd:	Oneness of Allah; Monotheism
Tawdīhul-Masā'il:	the book comprising answers to religious questions and problems according to the Islamic religious laws.

W

wājib (pl. *Wājibāt*):	1- (adi.): obligatory, incumbent 2- (n.) obligatory duty
wājibātuṣ-ṣalāt:	prayer duties or obligations; necessary preliminaries to be done while saying prayers. The most important points relative to *ṣalāt*
waqt:	time, a period of time
wuḍū':	performing ablution; ritual washing for *ṣalāt*; ritual ablution performed before prayer.

Z

Ẓuhr:	noon, midday

The glossary is Compiled and arranged by the editor.

Footnotes:

1. ” أرأيتم لوأن نهرا بباب أَحدِكم يغتسِلُ فيه كلَّ يومٍ خَمساً مـا يقول؟
ذلك يُبقى من درنه   قالوا: لايُبقي من درنه شيئًا!

قال: فذلك مثل الصلوات الخمس يمحو الله بها الخطايا. “

(Ṣaḥiḥul-Bukhāri, Vol. 9, Chapter 6).

2. The exact sign of the virtuous time for *Ṣalātul-'Aṣr* in the Islamic jurisprudential books, is the time when the eastbound shadow of everything equals its own size.

3. The decisive sign of the sunset in the horizon is that the pinkish evening twilight, seen after sunset in the one-half of the eastern part of the sky, disappears completely.

4- It means the time when the evening twilight disappears completely from the border of the western horizon of the sky.

5. If it is midnight and a man has not yet performed his *Ṣalātul-Maghrib* or *Ṣalātul-'Ishā'*, he must perform it before dawn without making his *niyyah* (intention) of either *adā'* (duly or in time), or *qaḍā'* (due at latertime)

6. *Adhān* and *iqāmah*, mentioned here, are as recorded in all the books of Shi'ah jurisprudence and are according to *aḥādith* of the infallible Imams (A.S.) after the prophet Muḥammad (S.A.), narrated in Shi`ah books on *aḥādith.* In "*Ar-Risālatul-'Amaliyyah li Tawḍiḥil-Masā'il*" (Treatise on practical Laws of Islam), Article No. (918), *adhān* and *iqāmah* have been mentioned in the same manner. Then in regard to the testification to the *wilāyah* (guardianship) of Imam 'Ali (A.S.), the following has been mentioned under Article (919)

"Ashhadu anna 'Aliyyan Waliyyul-Llāh."

is not part of *adhān* and *iqāmah,* but it is good to say it after "*Ashhadu anna Muḥammadan Rasūlu-Llāh*" with the intention of acquiring pleasure of Allah."

7. Under the following conditions, instead of *Wuḍū'* or with *Wuḍū'*

the whole body must be washed. This purification is called *ghusl.*

For men and women:

(a) After sexual intercourse or after seminal discharge.

(b) After touching the (human) corpse which has gone cold, and has not yet been given obligatory *ghusl.*

For women only

(c) At the end of ḥayḍ (menstrual period).

(d) At the end of nifās (discharge of blood after delivery)

(e) At the end of *istiḥāḍah,* which is extra-ordinary discharge of blood, at any undue time, whether fair or excessive.

Ghusl has two alternatives:

Either (a) *irtimāsi,* by which one should dip oneself once completely from head to feet; or (b) *tartībi* as follows: First wash the head, the neck, and hands, then half of the body on the right-hand side, and then wash the other half on the left-hand side. For *ghusl* it is enough if one washes his head and face, and then uses a wet towel, sponge or handkerchief for wiping half of the body on the right-hand side, and then the other half on the left-hand side.

Tayammum

If water is not available, or the worshipper, due to sickness or for any other reason, cannot utilize water for "*wuḍū*" or "*ghusl*", he, instead, can touch the clean soil, sand or stone, with the palms of his hands once and wipe his forehead with them. Then once again he must touch the clean soil, and or stone in the same manner, and draw (wipe) the left palm on the back of the right hand, and then the right palm on the back of the left hand, starting from the wrist and going slowly down to the finer-tips.

The Holy Qur'ān says:

... فَلَمْ تَجِدُوا مٰاءً فَتَيَمَّمُوا صَعيداً طَيِّباً فَامْسَحُوا بِوُجُوهِكُمْ وَ أَيْدِيكُمْ مِنْهُ مٰا يُرِيدُ اللّٰهُ لِيَجْعَلَ عَلَيْكُمْ مِنْ حَرَجٍ...

> *"...And if you cannot find water, betake yourselves to pure soil and wipe your faces and your hands with some of it. Allah does not desire to put on you any hardship..."*
>
> *(The Holy Qur'ān, 5: 6)*

8. Some of the *najāsāt* (impurities) with which the body and clothes of the worshipper must not be polluted are as follows:

- ❑ A dog.
- ❑ A pig.
- ❑ Urine and faeces of human beings, and those animals whose meat is *ḥarām* (prohibited) to eat, and whose blood gushes forth, when a blood vessel of theirs is cut.
- ❑ Human blood and semen.
- ❑ Blood and semen of all the animals whose blood gushes forth, whether their meat is *ḥarām* to eat or *ḥalāl* (permitted by Islam).
- ❑ Human corpse without ghuslul-mayyit (Islamic washing of the dead human body before burial)
- ❑ Those animal corpses whose blood gushes forth.

9. For *sujūd* the forehead must be placed on the soil, dust, stone, or the like, or things which grow out of the soil, but are not used for eating or clothing.

A small, round or oblong, earthen piece (*turbah*) carried and used for *sujūd* by us actually made from *ṭāhir* (pure) and clean soil.

10. This portion of prayer is called "*tashahhud* and *salām*". In *salām* of the *ṣalāt*, it suffices to say the last phrase only, i.e. "*As-salāmu 'alaykum wa raḥmatu-Llāhi wa barakātuh*".

11. In the first and second *rak'ahs* of the *Ṣalātuṣ-Ṣubḥ*, *Ṣalātul-Maghrib*, and *Ṣalātul-'Ishā'*, *Sūratul-Ḥamd* and another surah like *At-Tawḥīd* are recited aloud. And in the Ṣalātuẓ-*Ẓuhr* and *Ṣalātul'Aṣr*, these surahs are recited with a very low voice.

12. *Sīrat ibn Hishām*, vol. 1, p. 263.

13. *Ibid*, vol. 1, p. 282.

14. *Ibid*, vol. 4, p. 185.

15. *Ibid.*, vol. 2, p. 139

16. During the eclipse of the sun or of the moon, it is a common practice among many tribes to beat drums so as to frighten the giant

dragons which, according to their belief, come out while swallowing the sun or moon. These giant dragons, described mythically, may be possibly due to the shadow of the earth or the moon, which is the real cause of the eclipses. But there is no doubt that the beating of drums to scare the dragons is a fanciful and superstitious custom.

Attached Photos

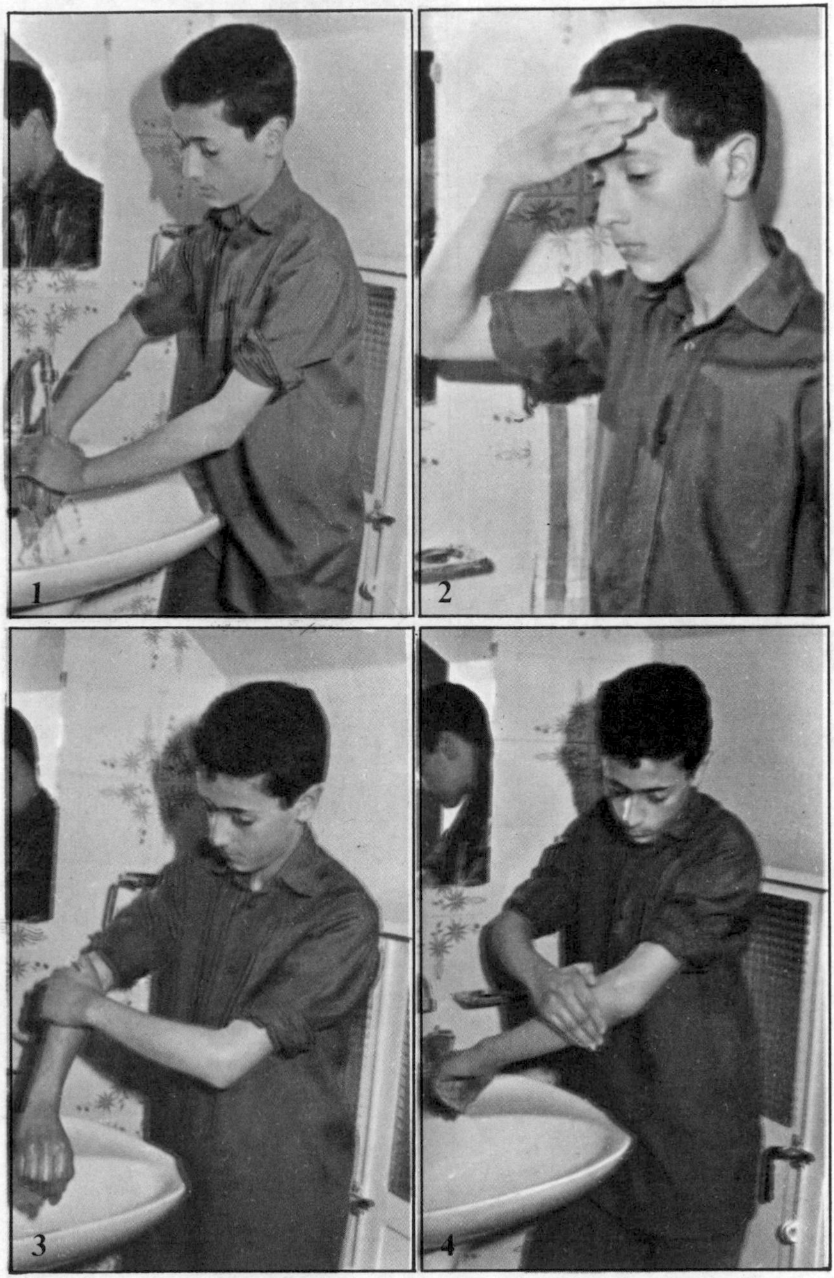
1
2
3
4

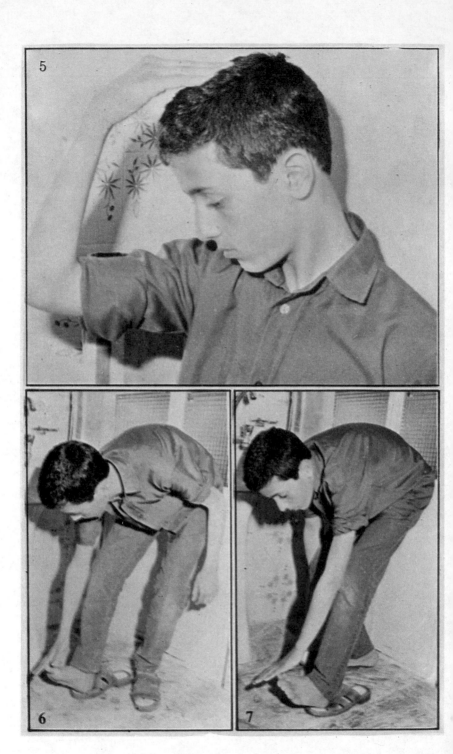

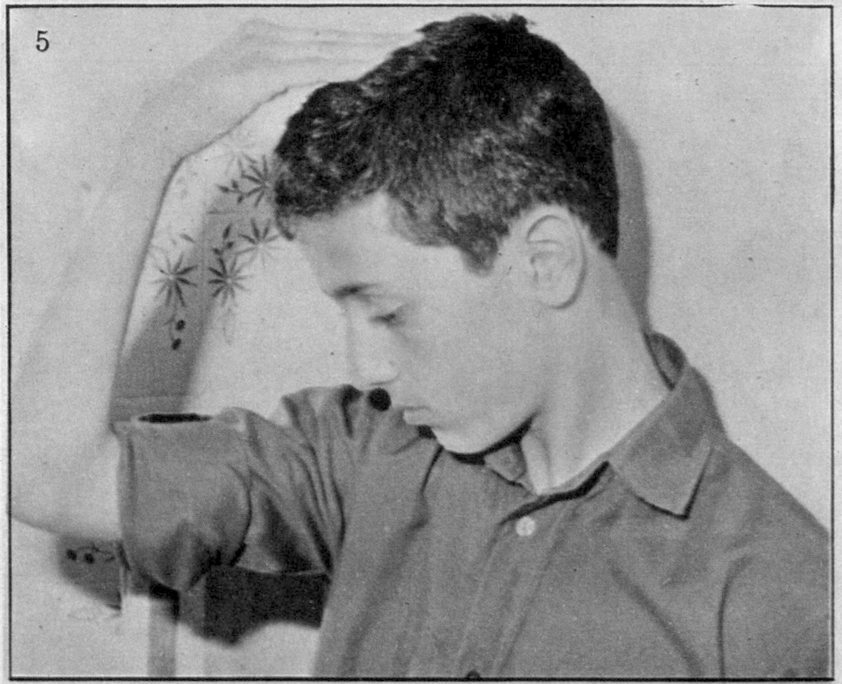

5

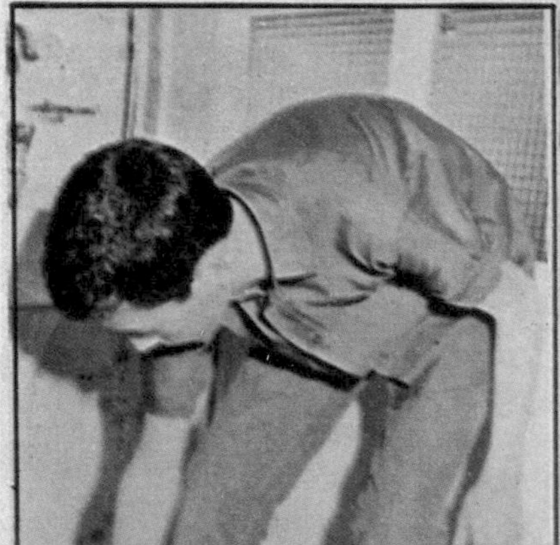

6

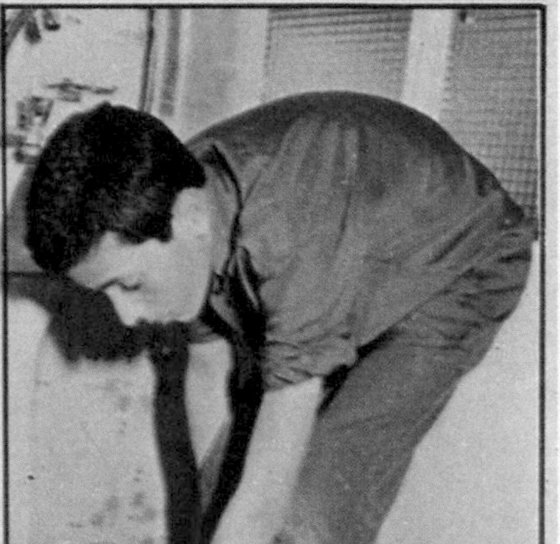

7

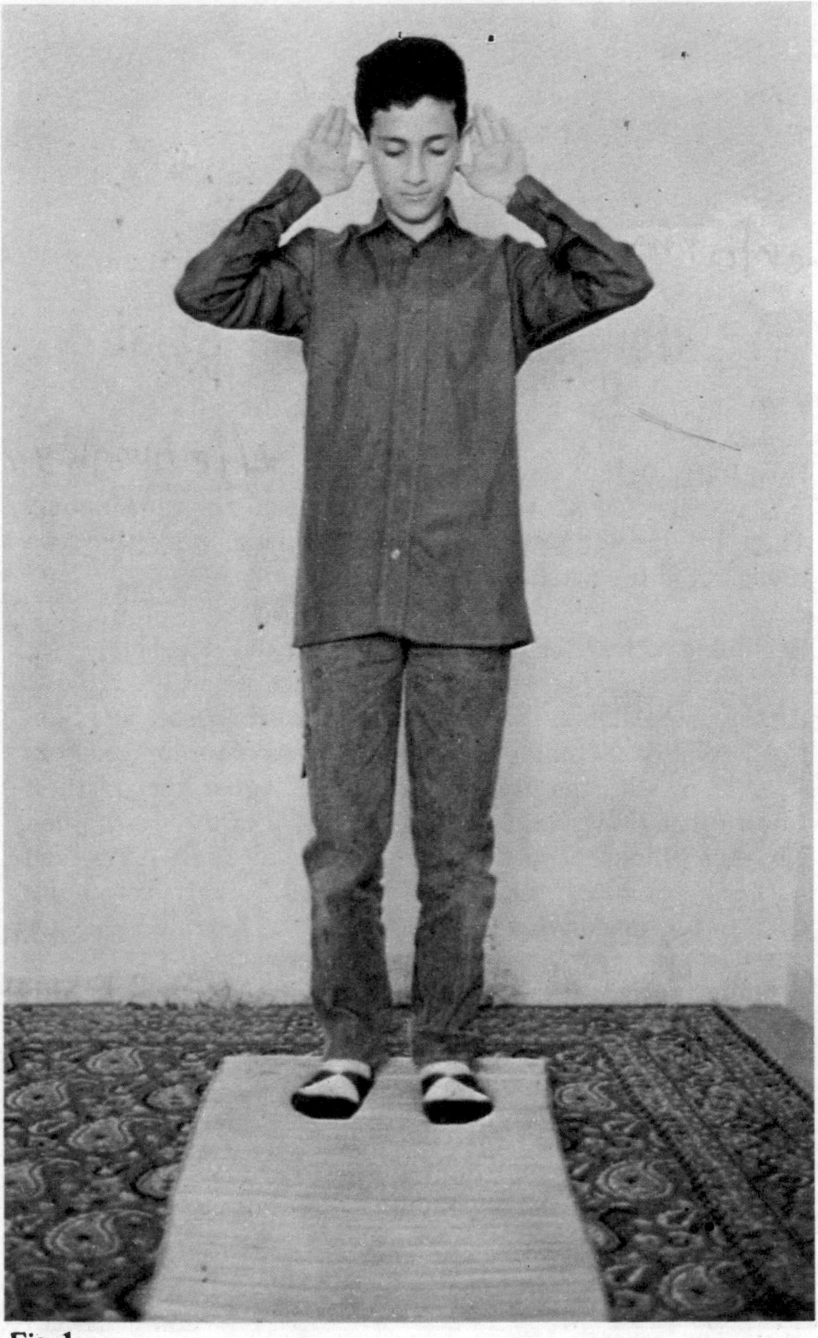

Fig 1

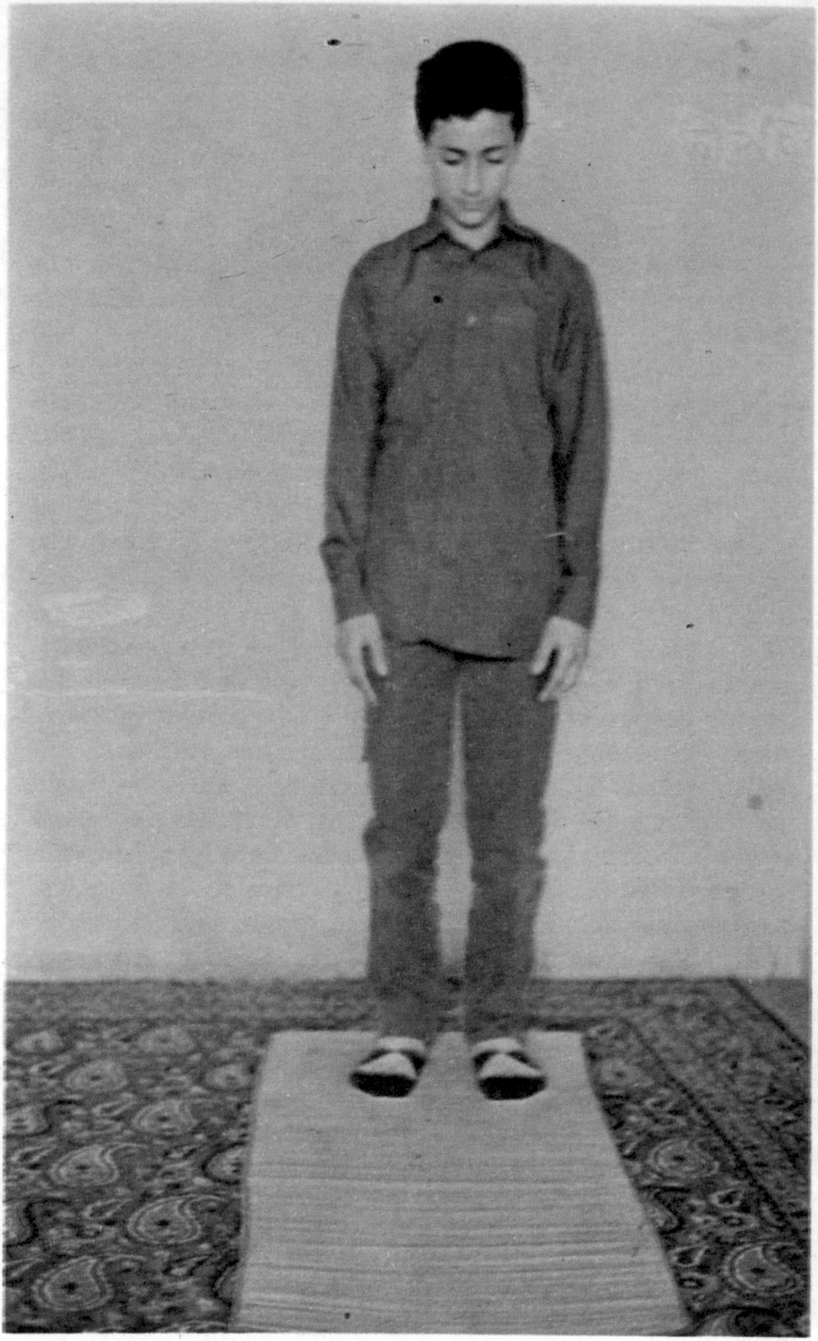

Fig 2

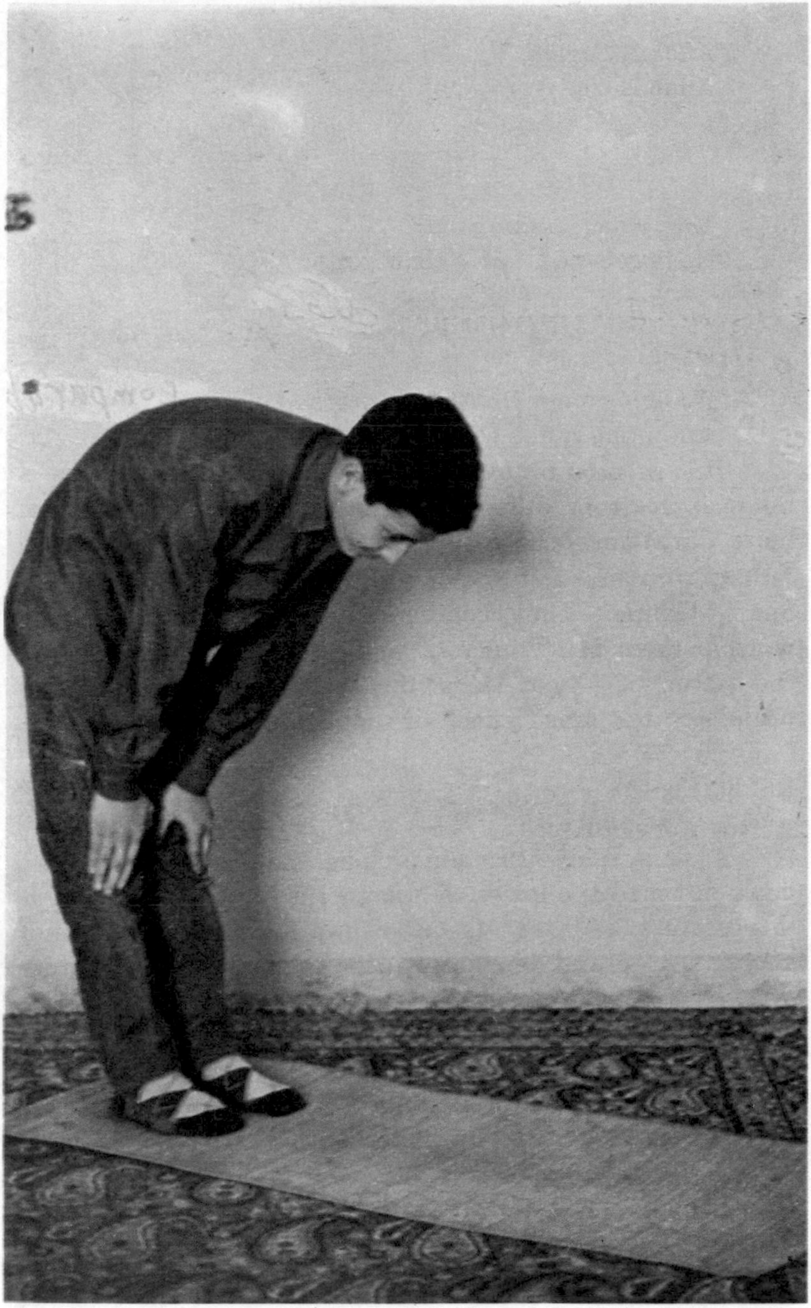

Fig 4

Fig 5

Fig 6